THE FOUNDING PRESIDENTS

A SOURCEBOOK ON THE U.S. PRESIDENCY

THE FOUNDING PRESIDENTS

A SOURCEBOOK ON THE U.S. PRESIDENCY

Edited by Carter Smith

AMERICAN ALBUMS FROM THE COLLECTIONS OF
THE LIBRARY OF CONGRESS

THE MILLBROOK PRESS, *Brookfield, Connecticut*

Cover: Detail from "Declaration of Independence in Congress, at the Independence Hall, Philadelphia." Painting by John Trumbull, 1818.

Title Page: "Georgetown and Federal City; or, the City of Washington." Hand-colored engraving published by Atkins & Nightingale, 1801.

Contents Page: "Seal of the United States of America." Drawing by Charles Thomson, 1782.

Back Cover: "The Home of Washington: Mount Vernon, Va." Lithograph by Currier & Ives, nineteenth century.

Library of Congress Cataloging-in-Publication Data

The founding presidents : a sourcebook on the U.S. presidency / edited by Carter Smith.
    p. cm. — (American albums from the collections of the Library of Congress)
    Includes bibliographical references and index.
    Summary: Uses a variety of contemporary materials to describe and illustrate the political and personal lives of the United States presidents from George Washington to James Monroe.
    ISBN 1-56294-357-X (lib. bdg.)
    1. Presidents—United States—History—Juvenile literature. 2. Presidents—United States—History—Sources—Juvenile literature. 3. United States—Politics and government—1783–1865—Juvenile literature. 4. United States—Politics and government—1783–1865—Sources—Juvenile literature. [1. Presidents—Sources. 2. United States—Politics and government—1783–1865—Sources.] I. Smith, C. Carter. II. Series.
E176.1.F77 1993
973'.099—dc20
[B]
                                        93-12751
                                          CIP
                                          AC

 Created in association with Media Projects Incorporated

C. Carter Smith, *Executive Editor*
Lelia Wardwell, *Managing Editor*
Kitty C. Benedict, *Principal Writer*
Charles A. Wills, *Manuscript Editor*
Lydia Link, *Designer*
Athena Angelos, *Picture Researcher*
John W. Kern, *Researcher*

The consultation of Bernard F. Reilly, Jr., Head Curator of the Prints and Photographs Division of the Library of Congress, is gratefully acknowledged.

Contents

Introduction   7

A Timeline of Major Events   10

Part I
The Challenge of Independence   19

Part II
A New Nation, a New Century   57

Resource Guide   94

Index   95

When Washington traveled to New York City on April 30, 1789, for the nation's first presidential inauguration, celebrations were held all along his journey. This Currier & Ives print shows Washington's reception in Trenton, New Jersey, where the women threw flowers in his path to honor his victory at Trenton during the Revolutionary War and wish him well in his new post.

Introduction

THE FOUNDING PRESIDENTS is one volume in a series published by The Millbrook Press titled AMERICAN ALBUMS FROM THE COLLECTIONS OF THE LIBRARY OF CONGRESS and the first of six books in the series, SOURCEBOOKS ON THE U.S. PRESIDENCY. This series chronicles the American presidency from George Washington through Bill Clinton.

The prints, broadsides, banners, manuscripts, and other ephemera reproduced in this volume reflect the extraordinary wealth of the Library's holdings of presidential documents. In fact, Thomas Jefferson's personal library formed the basis of the Library of Congress after the institution's original collections were burned by British troops during the War of 1812. Established long before the first presidential library, the Library of Congress also houses the papers of every American president from George Washington to Calvin Coolidge. These papers are supplemented in many instances by the personal memorabilia of presidents, including photographs, prints, and drawings.

The works shown here reveal a great deal about how Americans viewed their first presidents. Formal portraits of Washington, Jefferson, and their succes-sors were often designed to show the president in a favorable light, by conveying the particular philosophy or character which these individuals brought to office. Surviving political cartoons of these early years, on the other hand, indicate that caricature was an inescapable hazard of public life—even for such esteemed individuals as Thomas Jefferson and James Madison.

These pictorial documents also reveal how some of the first American presidents came to assume a symbolic importance long after their own lifetimes. Washington, in particular, in the years immediately preceding the Civil War, was seen as embodying the harmony of the federal Union, North and South. In the beginning of the twentieth century, as the United States moved uncertainly toward a role as a world power, artists invoked the memory of its first president as a statesman and a general.

The works reproduced here are a small but telling portion of the rich record of the American presidency, which is preserved today by the Library of Congress in its role as the nation's library.

BERNARD F. REILLY, JR.

During the first five presidencies, the territory of the United States of America changed significantly. At first, during the Revolutionary War, there were thirteen colonies, located along the Atlantic Coast. The early battles of the war were fought in the northern colonies (New York, New Jersey, and Massachusetts). Later the war was fought in the South, near George Washington's home in Virginia.

When America gained independence, the thirteen colonies became thirteen separate states, united under one government.

Under the terms of the Treaty of Paris of 1783, the United States' western boundary was the Mississippi River. This territory was gradually organized into separate states, starting with Kentucky (1792) and Tennessee (1796) during the presidency of John Adams.

President Thomas Jefferson authorized the Louisiana Purchase from France in 1803, which practically doubled the size of the country. He proceeded to send Lewis and Clark out to explore the vast new territory. Settlement and statehood would come later for the West—the priorities during the presidencies of James Monroe and James Madison concerned diplomatic troubles with Europe. Before the new nation moved into the new territory it had to secure its boundaries— through both treaty and war—from European interests.

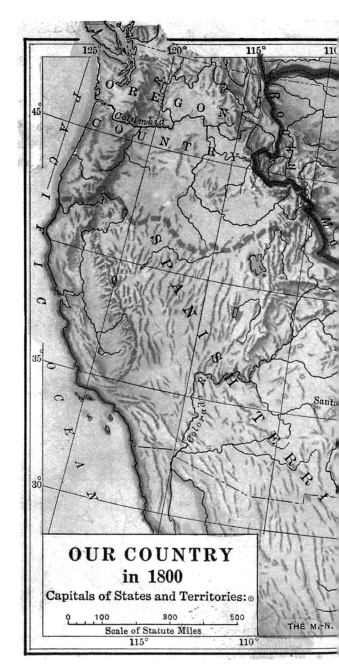

OUR COUNTRY
in 1800

Capitals of States and Territories: ⊙

Scale of Statute Miles

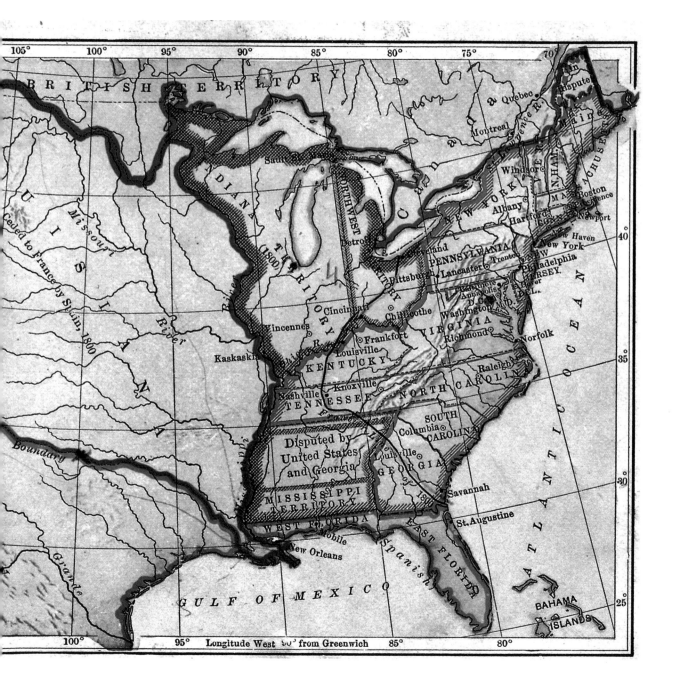

9

A TIMELINE OF MAJOR EVENTS
1776–1791

THE PRESIDENCY

1776 British general Sir William Howe defeats George Washington, commander in chief of the American forces, in the Battle of Long Island, one of many defeats the Continental Army suffers at the start of the Revolutionary War.
• In a daring surprise operation, Washington crosses the Delaware River to New Jersey, where he defeats Hessian troops at Trenton and drives the British out of Princeton in a key American victory.

1777 From the army's winter quarters in Valley Forge, Pennsylvania, Washington writes a letter to Congress, warning that unless the army receives new supplies of food and clothing, it must "starve, dissolve or disperse."

1781 Hungry and poorly clothed, American troops rebel against their superiors at Morristown, New Jersey, and march on Congress at Philadelphia. Washington sends in forces to crush the mutiny but later pardons the mutineers.
• Washington's army begins the siege of Yorktown, Virginia. In October, British general Charles Cornwallis surrenders his entire force, marking the end of British hopes for victory in America.

1783 At Newburgh, New York, Washington quells a movement among his officers to overthrow Congress and establish a monarchy with him as king.
• In a letter sent to all the states, Washington advocates support of a strong central government.

1787 New York becomes the capital.
• George Washington is unanimously elected to preside over the Constitutional Convention

THE AMERICAN SCENE

1776 In his pamphlet *Common Sense*, Thomas Paine attacks King George III and argues for colonial independence.
• Delegates to the Continental Congress in Philadelphia sign and approve the Declaration of Independence. Congress formally adopts the Declaration in July.

1777 The Continental Congress authorizes a "United States" flag, which has thirteen stars and thirteen red and white stripes.

1781 Congress ratifies the Articles of Confederation and Perpetual Union.

1783 The Revolutionary War ends when the U.S. and Britain sign the Treaty of Paris.

1784 James Madison argues for the separation of church and state in a pamphlet titled *Remonstrances Against Religious Assessments.*

1786 Daniel Shays leads a band of rebellious farmers in a march on the arsenal in Springfield, Massachusetts, to protest high taxes and inflation. The rebellion is put down, and Shays is indicted for treason.
• Representatives from five states meet in Annapolis, Maryland, to discuss reforming the Articles of Confederation. This meet

The Declaration of Independence is announced

Crest of the United States

when it meets in Philadelphia.

1789 George Washington becomes the first president of the United States; John Adams is vice president.
•Washington commissions Major Pierre Charles L'Enfant, a French artist, designer, and architect, to design the plan for the nation's new capital in Washington, D.C.
• One week after his inauguration as president, George Washington is the guest of honor at the first inaugural ball.
• The first department of the executive branch of government—the Department of Foreign Affairs, later renamed the Department of State— is created by Congress. Thomas Jefferson is selected by Washington to head the agency.
• At Congress's urging, President Washington declares November 26 a national day of Thanksgiving for the Constitution. This marks the first celebration of Thanksgiving as a national holiday.

1790 The temporary federal capital is moved from New York City to Philadelphia.

1791 President Washington signs a bill creating the first Bank of the United States, which is to be established in Philadelphia.

---

ing sets the stage for the Constitutional Convention the following year.

1787 *The Federalist Papers* are published in New York. This series of essays by James Madison, Alexander Hamilton, and John Jay urges ratification of the Constitution.
• The Northwest Ordinance organizes a government for the territory around the Ohio River and the Great Lakes. Settlement of the region begins with the founding of Marietta, in present-day Ohio, in 1788.

1788 The United States Constitution takes effect after ratification by nine of the thirteen states.

1789 Inventor John Fitch demonstrates his steamboat at Philadelphia.

1790 The nation's first census shows the population at almost 4 million, including about 700,000 slaves and

Samuel Slater's water-powered textile mill

60,000 free blacks.
• The first water-powered textile mill in the United States, built by English immigrant Samuel Slater, begins operating in Pawtucket, Rhode Island.

1791 The ten amendments known as the Bill of Rights are added to the Constitution.

UNITED STATES HISTORY

1792 The Republican-Democratic Party is formed to oppose the Federalists and represent the rights of farmers and those who favor a less centralized government. Thomas Jefferson emerges as the Party's leading spokesman.
• George Washington, running virtually unopposed, is reelected for a second term as president. Adams is reelected vice president.

1793 Washington announces a Proclamation of Neutrality which he hopes will protect the United States from the war between France and Britain.

1794 Washington leads 15,000 troops to quell the Whiskey Rebellion, an uprising of Pennsylvania grain farmers who refuse to pay the federal tax on the manufacture of whiskey.

1795 Washington refuses to accept a third term as president.
• Congress ratifies John Jay's Treaty with Great Britain. The treaty calls for British forces to evacuate the Great Lakes region.
• In his farewell address, Washington warns of the evils of political parties and entangling foreign alliances, and of the dangers of

Bank of the United States, Philadelphia

THE AMERICAN SCENE

1792 The nation's first stock exchange is organized in New York City.

1793 Eli Whitney invents the cotton gin, revolutionizing agriculture in the southern United States.
• Over 4,000 people die in Philadelphia from yellow fever. African Americans, who are thought to be immune from the disease, are hired to treat the sick.

1794 Congress passes the Neutrality Act, which forbids American citizens to fight in a foreign army against a nation at peace with the U.S.
• Susanna Haswell Rowson publishes the first American bestseller, *Charlotte Temple, a Tale of Truth.*
• Charles Willson Peale founds the Philadelphia Museum, the first independent museum in America.

• The sixty-mile-long Lancaster Turnpike, connecting Philadelphia with Lancaster, Pennsylvania, opens to traffic. It is the nation's first major inter-city road.

1796 Gilbert Stuart paints a portrait of George Washington. It becomes the most famous depiction of the nation's first president.

1798 Congress passes the Alien and Sedition Acts. The first gives the president power to deport foreigners, and the second makes dissent a federal offense.
• Congress repeals all treaties with France, ordering the U.S. Navy to capture French ships, beginning an undeclared naval war.

1798 Inventor Eli Whitney pioneers the use of interchangeable parts in the manufacture of weapons for the U.S. government.
1799 The U.S. Navy wins its first victory

an overgrown military.
• The U.S. and Spain sign the Treaty of San Lorenzo, which establishes the boundary between the U.S. and Spain's North American territory. The treaty also guarantees American vessels the right to travel on the Mississippi River.

1797 Federalist and former vice president John Adams is inaugurated as the country's sec-

ond president after defeating Democratic-Republican Thomas Jefferson by three votes. Jefferson becomes vice president as runner-up, according to the electoral rules established by the Constitution.

1798 President Adams exposes the XYZ Affair. The French had tried to obtain more than $10 million from the American negotiators as a bribe to conduct diplomatic talks with the U.S.

1799 President Adams reopens negotiations with France in an effort to avoid war.

1800 Washington, D.C. becomes the national capital.
• The presidential election results in the defeat of John Adams and a tie between Republicans Thomas Jefferson and Aaron Burr; the House of Representatives elects Jefferson president and Burr vice president.
• Congress divides the Northwest Ter-

ritory into the Indiana and Ohio territories. Eventually, the states of Illinois, Indiana, Michigan, Ohio, and Wisconsin are created from the Northwest Territory.
• The U.S. and French governments sign the Treaty of Morfontaine, ending two years of undeclared naval war between the two nations.

---

when the American frigate, the *Constellation*, seizes the French ship, *L'Insurgente*, in the West Indies.
• Shoemakers in Philadelphia strike in the first organized labor protest in the U.S.
• Hannah Adams's book, *A Summary History of New England*, is published, making Adams the first American woman to earn a living by writing.
• The New York legislature passes a law calling for the gradual emancipa-

tion (freeing) of the slaves in the states. Most of the Northern states have outlawed slavery by this time.
• In response to the Alien and

Sedition Acts, Thomas Jefferson and James Madison draft the Virginia and Kentucky Resolutions. The resolutions argue that individual states have the

right to nullify (declare invalid) federal laws they consider unconstitutional.

1800 The Library of Congress is created.
• The U.S. census cites the population at 5.3 million. Virginia is the most populous state.
• One thousand slaves, led by George Prosser, revolt in an attempt to end slavery in Virginia. The leaders are caught and hanged.

Naval heroes of the Revolutionary War

A TIMELINE OF MAJOR EVENTS
1801–1812

UNITED STATES HISTORY

1801 Before leaving office, John Adams appoints Federalist John Marshall chief justice of the Supreme Court and names the "midnight judges," also Federalists. These appointments are vital to the Federalists, who are losing control of the legislative and executive branches of government.

1802 President Jefferson and Secretary of the Treasury Albert Gallatin implement policies to reduce the national debt, military spending, and the size of government.

1803 The 12th Amendment to the Constitution is passed, requiring separate balloting for president and vice president. As a result, the runner-up in an election no longer automatically becomes vice president.
• Jefferson buys the 800,000-square-mile Louisiana Territory from the French for $14.5 million. The Louisiana Purchase doubles the size of the United States.

1804 Jefferson commissions an exploration of the territory acquired through the Louisiana Purchase. Meriwether Lewis and William Clark lead the expedition. In November 1805, their party reaches the Pacific Ocean.

1805 After defeating Federalist Charles Pinckney by a landslide, Thomas Jefferson is inaugurated for a second term as president; he urges Congress to eliminate Federalist taxes on the working class. He also proposes that any revenue lost by this measure be made up by a luxury tax on the wealthy.

1806 Jefferson asks Congress to ban the African slave trade. Congress complies

THE AMERICAN SCENE

1801 The *New York Evening Post* is published by Alexander Hamilton and John Jay.
• American inventor Robert Fulton builds the *Nautilus*, a human-powered submarine that uses a snorkel to obtain air while the vessel is running under water.
• The first suspension bridge is built, at Uniontown, Pennsylvania.
• When the U.S. government stops its customary payment of bribes to prevent attacks on American ships in the Mediterranean Sea, the North African state of Tripoli declares war on the United States. In a conflict that lasts until 1805, the U.S. Navy forces Tripoli to back down.

1802 Congress establishes the U.S. Military Academy at West Point, New York.
• John Chapman, better known as

Meriwether Lewis

Johnny Appleseed, begins planting apple trees in Licking County, Ohio. His planting eventually yields close to 100,000 square miles of fruit-bearing trees across the country.

1806 *A Compendious Dictionary of the English Language* is published by Noah Webster; it contains many words unique to the American language that had not formerly appeared in British dictionaries.

1807 Former vice president Aaron Burr is tried for treason for his part in a scheme to form a western empire with the Span-

the following year, but illegal trade continues.
• Jefferson refuses to accept a third term as president.

1807 Responding to British and French assaults on American merchant ships, Jefferson asks Congress to pass the Embargo and Non-Importation Acts. These laws, which prohibit all foreign trade into or out of U.S. ports, cause a nationwide economic depression.

James Madison

1809 Conceding that the Embargo Act has badly damaged the U.S. economy, Jefferson asks Congress to pass the Non-Inter-course Act, which permits U.S. ships to trade with all countries except for England and France.
• James Madison, Jefferson's hand-picked successor, is inaugurated as the nation's fourth president after defeating Federalist Charles Pinckney. George Clinton begins his second term as vice president.

1810 President Madison annexes part of western Florida (which will later become the states of Alabama and Mississippi) by signing a presidential proclamation.

1812 Although he advocates peace, President Madison is persuaded by a group of young congressmen (known as "war hawks") to ask Congress to declare war on Britain. Congress complies, and the War of 1812 begins.

---

ish; he is acquitted, and leaves the country to avoid prosecution for the killing of Alexander Hamilton in a duel.
• The first commercial steamboat trip is made by Robert Fulton's *Clermont* up the Hudson River toward Albany, New York.

1809 John James Audubon paints detailed studies of birds and traces their migration.

1810 The Boston Philharmonic Society is founded; it is the first regular orchestra in the country.
• The census shows that the population of the United States has jumped 36 percent since 1800. It now totals over 7 million.

1811 Indian tribes east of the Mississippi form a confederation under the Shawnee chief Tecumseh. The confederation's attempt to reclaim Indian lands fails when it loses a battle with General William Henry Harrison's troops near Tippecanoe Creek in the Indiana territory.
• Four hundred slaves, led by free Haitian Charles Deslondes, revolt in Louisiana, destroying several plantations and killing two whites. The militia kills sixty-six slaves and publicly displays their heads along the roadways.
• Construction begins on the Cumberland Road, the first major highway funded by the federal government.

The road eventually runs from Cumberland, Maryland, to Vandalia, Illinois.

1812 The American warship *Constitution* ("Old Ironsides") wins a major victory for the U.S. Navy when it destroys the British frigate *Guerrière*.
• Congress authorizes $50,000 in assistance to victims of a Central American earthquake—the first foreign aid in American history.

A TIMELINE OF MAJOR EVENTS
1813–1823

UNITED STATES HISTORY

1813 James Madison is inaugurated for a second term. Democratic-Republican Elbridge Gerry is elected vice president.
• The British burn Washington, D.C., forcing President Madison to flee the city.

1814 Madison signs the Treaty of Ghent, ending the War of 1812.

1817 In his last act as president, Madison vetoes a congressional act to pay for major roadways and canals to connect the Eastern seaboard with the West.
• James Monroe is inaugurated as the fifth president after easily defeating Federalist Rufus King. Daniel D. Tompkins is elected as his vice president.
• After observing the enthusiasm and unity of the American people in their desire to build a great nation under President Monroe, a newspaperman writes that Monroe's election has ushered in the "Era of Good Feelings."
• Congress commissions artist John Trumbull to create a series of paintings to decorate the Capitol. Trumbull's large-scale paintings of scenes from American history include *The Signing of the Declaration of Independence*, completed in 1818.

1817–18 War breaks out between

Washington, D.C., 1817

THE AMERICAN SCENE

1813 The nickname "Uncle Sam" is used for the first time in a newspaper in Troy, New York.

1814 American general Andrew Jackson defeats the Creek Indians at Horseshoe Bend, Alabama, forcing them to give up 22 million acres of land.
• Attorney Francis Scott Key composes the famous "Star Spangled Banner" after the defeat of the British at Baltimore, Maryland.

1815 Unaware that a peace treaty has been signed, British troops unsuccessfully attack 4,500 Americans (mostly Southern frontiersmen led by General Andrew Jackson) near New Orleans.

1816 The national debt reaches an all-time high of $127 million.

1817 Minister Thomas Gallaudet opens the first American school for the deaf, the American Asylum, in Connecticut.

1818 The Convention of 1818 sets the border between the U.S. and Canada at the 49th parallel.

1819 A financial panic sweeps the country, triggering the failure of many state banks and causing a nationwide economic depression.

• The Florida Purchase Treaty, negotiated by Secretary of State John Quincy Adams, is signed. The treaty cedes West Florida to the United States; in return, the U.S. agrees to settle the legal claims of the U.S. citizens against the Spanish government.

1820 Under the Missouri Compromise, Missouri is admitted as a slave state and Maine as a free state, thereby preserving

U.S. forces and Seminole Indians in U.S.-controlled East Florida. During the fighting, General Andrew Jackson leads American forces into west Florida, which is still Spanish territory, causing an international incident.

1818 President and Mrs. Monroe hold a public reception; guests call the president's house the White House because of the white paint used to cover fire damage from the War of 1812.

1819 In the landmark Supreme Court case of *McCulloch* v. *Maryland*, Chief Justice John Marshall establishes the doctrine of implied powers—the idea that the federal government's authority is not limited solely to the powers specified in the Constitution. Marshall's ruling paves the way for a greater role for the federal government, and the Supreme Court in American life.

1821 After winning a decisive victory over Secretary of State John Quincy Adams, James Monroe is inaugurated for a second term. Vice President Daniel D. Tompkins is also reelected.

1822 President Monroe recognizes the revolutionary government of the Mexican Republic, and asks Congress to establish diplomatic relations with other newly formed Latin American republics.

1823 James Monroe presents the Monroe Doctrine to Congress. In it, he warns European nations not to interfere in the affairs of countries in the Western Hemisphere. The doctrine is Monroe's most significant achievement as president.

---

the balance between free and slave states.
• The New York Stock Exchange becomes the nation's leading stock exchange.
• The fourth census establishes the population at 10 million, with 2 million people now living west of the Allegheny Mountains. New York City is now the nation's largest city.
• Washington Irving's book, *Rip Van Winkle: The Legend of Sleepy Hollow*,

General Andrew Jackson in west Florida

causes a sensation when it is published in the *New York Evening Post*.

1821 The first public high school in the U.S. is established in Boston, Massachusetts.

1823 Proponents of abolition begin the Underground Railroad, a network which helps escaped slaves from Southern plantations get to the North.
• The U.S. economy begins to recover from the depression of 1819, strengthened by the growth of manufacturing and domestic and foreign trade.

Part I
The Challenge of Independence

The Second Continental Congress met in Philadelphia's State House in 1775 before the beginning of the Revolutionary War. After the Declaration of Independence was signed here on July 6, 1776, the graceful Georgian building became known as Independence Hall

The election of George Washington as the first president of the United States, in February 1789, marked a turning point not only in American history but in world history, too. The eighteenth century was a time when monarchs ruled most nations, often without any limitations on their power. But in the newly independent United States, a different kind of leader had emerged—one who was elected by, and responsible to, the people he governed. The delegates to the Constitutional Convention in 1787 saw that America would need a strong national leader, but one whose power would be balanced by Congress and the courts.

Washington was living happily at Mount Vernon, his Virginia plantation, when he received news of his election. On his way to the capital, New York City, he was greeted by crowds of enthusiastic people in every town. Only thirteen years earlier, the American colonists had astonished the world by launching a rebellion against Great Britain. Amazingly, the American colonies, under Washington's military leadership, had won their independence.

While Washington led the military struggle, John Adams of Massachusetts took a leading role in the political side of the conflict. He, too, was on his way to New York, to be sworn in as the nation's first vice president. Eight years later, Adams would succeed Washington as the nation's second president.

WASHINGTON'S EARLY YEARS

The man whom Thomas Jefferson called "a wise, a good and a great man" was born February 22, 1732, in Westmoreland County, Virginia. George Washington's father, Augustine, was a successful Virginia planter who had three children, Lawrence, Augustine, Jr., and Jane, from his first marriage. Washington's family was typical of the planter class, owning some six to ten thousand acres.

Young George learned about horse riding, farming, shooting, and hunting. He spent a lot of time with his brother Lawrence, who had inherited Mount Vernon, a family plantation, after their father died in 1743. Young George went to many evening parties and dances at nearby plantations, where he met the important people of the colony. His formal education was limited, and he never went to college.

When he was sixteen, Washington was hired by a prominent Virginia family to survey their lands in Shenandoah Valley. The following year, 1749, he was appointed surveyor of Culpeper County, Virginia. He helped lay out the city now known as Alexandria, just outside the nation's capital, and bought almost 1,500 acres of frontier land for himself.

In the 1750s, Lawrence Washington fell ill. George accompanied his beloved brother to the West Indies in the hope that he would recover, but Lawrence died in 1752. George himself caught smallpox, a dreaded disease at the time, but survived.

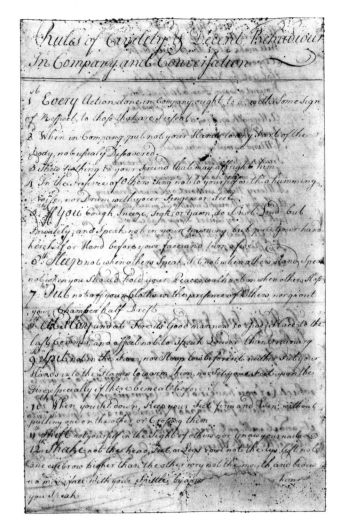

In colonial times, children were held to high standards of behavior, obedience, and politeness. Young George Washington wrote down these "Rules of Civility and Decent Behavior in Company and Conversation" (above). Altogether, there are 110 rules in his notebook (these are the first twelve). Number five reads: "If you Cough, Sneeze, Sigh or Yawn, do it not Loud, but Privately . . . put your Handkerchief or Hand before your face and turn aside."

In a page from George Washington's surveying notebook (right), the thirteen-year-old copied out a definition of surveying: "It is the Art of Measuring Land and it consists of 3 Parts. 1st. the Going round and Measuring a Piece of Wood Land. 2d. Plotting the Same and 3d To find the Content thereof and first how to Measure a Piece of Land." In 1747, Washington, then fifteen, mapped out his brother Lawrence's turnip field.

Washington's birthplace at Pope's Creek, Virginia, is seen in the distance in this engraving (below), based on a painting by J. G. Chapman. The house was built by Augustine Washington for his first wife and their three children. After his first wife died, Augustine married Mary Ball in 1731, and the next year George was born. In 1779, the house was destroyed by fire, but by then the family had already moved to the future site of Mount Vernon. Mary Ball died in 1789.

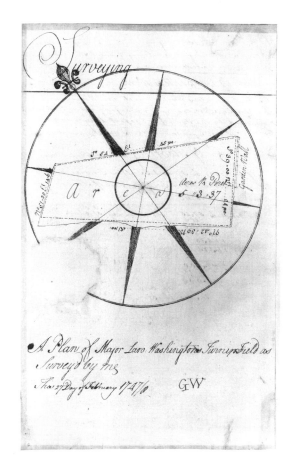

WASHINGTON THE SOLDIER

Two great colonial powers, France and Britain, struggled for control of the American frontier west of the Appalachian Mountains in the 1750s. As an officer in the Virginia militia, Washington was sent into the Ohio River Valley in 1753 to warn the French to leave the region. It was a challenging mission for the inexperienced soldier, but he handled it well.

Early the next year, Washington was promoted to lieutenant colonel. He was ordered to build a fort at Fort Duquesne (now Pittsburgh) on the Ohio River. After construction was finished, Washington ambushed a French patrol in the first skirmish of what became the French and Indian Wars. A few weeks later on July 4, 1754, a French force defeated Washington and his troops and took control of Fort Duquesne. The French commander allowed him to lead his men back to Williamsburg, Virginia.

In June 1755, Washington served as an aide to British general Edward Braddock, who was leading an expedition to recapture Fort Duquesne from the French. When Braddock was mortally wounded in a surprise attack, Washington bravely led the survivors out of danger.

After the British withdrew from the Virginia frontier, the Virginia Assembly asked Washington to defend the 350-mile Virginia border. It was an impossible job, complicated by lack of money and troops, but it prepared Washington for the difficulties he would face in the Revolutionary War.

After his 1754 defeat, Washington resigned his commission. In the spring of 1755, he was back in uniform as an aide to General Braddock. Washington is shown mounted on a horse with his sword raised in this illustration (above), with Braddock's forces in the Virginia wilderness. They were attacked by French and Indian soldiers at the Monongahela River. The British soldiers panicked and fled, leaving 300 dead behind. Washington managed to lead the remaining troops safely back to Fort Cumberland, Maryland.

Washington kept records of all his expenses as an officer, claiming refunds for what he spent on "Cleaning my Pistols," "Milk," and "Washing," as shown here (right) in one of his expense accounts. He also recorded his experiences in battle. After Washington's first skirmish with the French and Indians in May 1754, he wrote, "I heard the bullets whistle, and, believe me, there is something charming in the sound."

	Contra	C.º	
1755	By Sum brought forward	211 . 16 . 1½	
	By Cash to my Bro. John supposd to be as they were	21 . 13 . 4	
	5 dubloons		
May 28	By a large Bay Horse of Saml M.ᶜRoberts	10 . __ . 6	
29	By Thomas for a Bell	0 . 5 . 0	
	By Ditto gave	11 . 6	
	By Ropes Gee	5	
June	By altering my Calesh	1 . 8	
	By Captain Ormes Servant	1 . 3	
	By Cresaps acc.ᵗ	2 . 16 . 10	
	By Mr. Shirley's Servant	1 . 3	
10	By John Albon	10 . __	
	By making a black Stock	4	
	By Cash gave to	5	
13	By Washing	10 . 8	
	By Tho.ˢ Thomas	2 . 10½	
17	By Col. Burtons Servant	2 . 10½	
27	By Cleaning my Pistols	3 . 1½	
July 2	By 8 days attendance of a Nurse in my Sickness	__ . 0	
4	By Milk	5 . 9	
	By 3 pair Hopples	9 . __	
21	By M.ʳ Hawthorn for a Mattrass	1 . 2 . 6½	
22	By Washing	5 . 9	
	By Thomas Thomas for a Horse	2 . 1 . 6	
	By Joseph Bunnan - Batman	5 . 9	
	By Smith for shoeing my Horse	1 . 3	
23	By Expences at M.ᶜCrackens	5 . 9	
24	By Jeff. Oliver	5 . 4	
	By Expences at Winchester	2 . 6	
	By Ditto at Edward Thompsons	5 . 9	
27	By Water Mellons	1 . 3	
31	By 20 Bushels of Oats	2 . __	
Aug.ᵗ 1	By M.ʳ Posey	4 . 6 . 8	
	By my Brothers Serv.ᵗ 1/3. By Bosley inf.ᵗ for 2/6/3 .	7 . 6	
	By M.ʳ Dalton for Paying Belt & Meads acc.ᵗ	4 . 6 . 0	
	By Sum carried Over	£466 . 12 . 3½	

MARTHA WASHINGTON

In March 1759, after leaving military service, Washington met and became engaged to Martha Dandridge Custis, the daughter of a tobacco planter. Born June 2, 1731, near Williamsburg, Virginia, Martha had married Daniel Parke Custis at age seventeen. They had four children, two who died in childhood and two, John and Martha, who lived into adulthood. When he died in 1757, Custis left his wife 17,000 acres of land and hundreds of slaves, making her one of the richest women in Virginia.

Martha was a lively and attractive woman whose easy manners endeared her to everyone she met. Abigail Adams called her "one of those unassuming characters which create Love and Esteem." Washington and Martha were married January 9, 1759. Although they had no children of their own, Washington adopted Martha's children.

During the eight years Washington was commander in chief of the Continental Army, Martha often made long, difficult journeys to his winter headquarters. There, she nursed sick soldiers, copied his correspondence, and cheered up the wives of the other officers. Although, like her husband, she preferred the life of a private citizen, she cheerfully performed her duties as the nation's First Lady after George Washington was elected president in 1789. Outliving her husband by only two years, she died at Mount Vernon on May 22, 1802, aged seventy.

Widowhood made Martha Dandridge Custis (1731–1802; above) the owner of vast acres of land and a plantation on the Pamunkey River near Williamsburg, Virginia. This experience later helped Martha become an excellent manager of the huge Mount Vernon estate.

At her marriage to George Washington on January 9, 1759, Martha Dandridge Custis, at twenty-seven, was a few months older than George. The wedding, shown in this lithograph (right) based on a painting by J. B. Stearns, was held at her plantation, where the couple decided to spend their honeymoon.

Martha Parke Custis (1756–72; right), called Patsy, was the second of Martha Washington's two surviving children by Daniel Parke Custis. Washington was a kind stepfather to his two stepchildren. Patsy, shown here in a portrait by John Wollaston, was subject to epileptic fits. Her mother and stepfather tried to get the best medical help for her, and traveled to Berkeley Springs (now Bath), Maryland, hoping that the spring waters would be good for her health. But in 1773, at the age of seventeen, Patsy died suddenly at Mount Vernon.

WASHINGTON: PLANTER AND PATRIOT

When Washington inherited the Mount Vernon plantation (right) from his half brother's wife in 1754, it was run-down and in need of much repair. In 1759, before bringing his bride to Mount Vernon, shown in this print by Currier & Ives, Washington added a story to the original house.

In this 1853 lithograph (below), from a painting by J. B. Stearns, Washington is shown supervising the work on his plantation. He was a careful overseer of his land, riding out over the estate every day. He was also a scientific farmer, keeping up-to-date on the latest advances in agriculture and experimenting with soils, seeds, fertilizers, and crop rotation.

With his bride, twenty-seven-year-old George Washington happily took up his life as the owner of Mount Vernon, where he remained for fifteen years. He enlarged the house, built a flour mill, and experimented with raising sheep and growing grapes. Martha supervised the children's lessons, the dairy, the smokehouse, the laundry, and the kitchen. They entertained frequently and attended balls, weddings, card parties, and fox hunts.

When Britain began to raise taxes and control the colonies' trade in the 1760s, the Americans began to oppose British rule. At first, Washington was more concerned with his private affairs than with those of the colonies, but in 1769, he proposed a boycott of British goods, writing to his friend George Mason that "our lordly masters in Great Britain" wanted the "deprivation of American freedom."

When rebels in Boston protested British taxes on imported tea with their famous Boston Tea Party, Washington was spurred into action. In 1774, he told the first Virginia Provincial Convention that he would "raise 1,000 men" at his own expense to march to the aid of the Bostonians. The offer was turned down, but he was elected a delegate to the First Continental Congress in Philadelphia in 1774, and to the Second Continental Congress in 1775. The purpose of the Continental Congress was to decide the course of action to be taken by the thirteen colonies against Britain.

WASHINGTON TAKES COMMAND

Washington arrived in Philadelphia on May 9, 1775, just after news arrived of the clash between British troops and colonial militia at Lexington and Concord, Massachusetts. The conflict against Britain had now become open war. John Adams (1735–1826) of Massachusetts nominated Washington to be commander of the American forces. Washington accepted.

The 14,000 soldiers of the Continental Army (so named because it consisted of men from all the colonies) were more a crowd of undisciplined men than an army. But Washington was determined to show that the Americans could fight and win. In March 1776, Washington drove the British out of Boston.

The British attacked New York in July. Washington attempted to defend Brooklyn and Manhattan, but the British overwhelmed his forces. He marched to White Plains in Westchester County, then crossed the Hudson River into New Jersey, finally retreating into Pennsylvania. Desperate for a victory, Washington led 2,400 men across the icy Delaware River on December 26, 1776, in a successful surprise attack on the sleeping Hessian soldiers in Trenton, New Jersey. (The Hessians were Germans hired by the British.) The victory at Trenton gave the Revolutionary cause a new lease on life.

In this French engraving (above) by Noel Le Mire, George Washington is shown in his general's uniform. He holds a sheaf of papers in his right hand—among them copies of the Declaration of Independence and the Treaty of Alliance with France. Behind Washington, a servant tends to his horse. (The servant's moorish costume is the artist's invention and is not historically accurate.)

When John Adams nominated Washington to command the Continental Army in June 1775, Washington jumped from his seat in Federal Hall, Philadelphia, and left the room. He remained absent while the election took place the next day. This is the document Congress issued (opposite, top) that named him "Commander in Chief of the United Colonies."

On June 23, 1775, Washington set out from Philadelphia for Boston with major generals Charles Lee and Philip Schuyler. He set up his headquarters in Cambridge, Massachusetts. On July 3, he officially took command of the army, as shown in this nineteenth-century engraving (right). In a letter to his brother, Washington described the troops as "a mixed multitude of People here, under very little discipline, order, or Government."

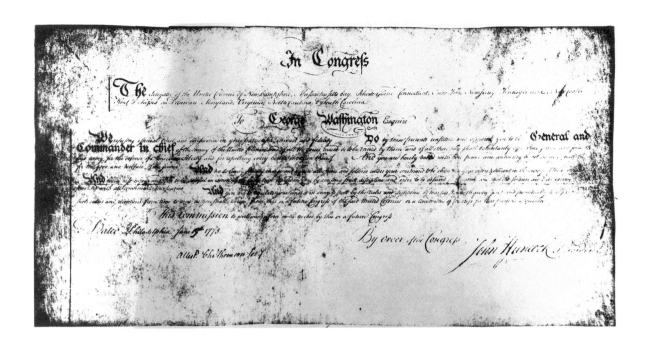

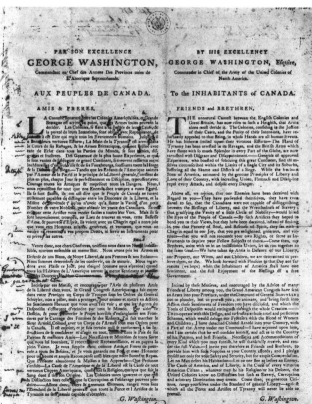

The valor of the new American navy was shown by the exploits of men like Scottish-born captain John Paul Jones (1747–92), whose ship, the Bonhomme Richard is shown in this engraving (above). During a moonlit battle off the coast of England on September 23, 1779, Captain Richard Pearson of the British warship Serapis demanded Jones's surrender. Jones replied, "I have not yet begun to fight," and went on to capture the Serapis.

Several American leaders hoped Canada, a former possession of France, would join the colonies in their rebellion against Britain. In 1775, Washington sent this letter (left), printed in French and English, urging the Canadians to unite with the Americans. "We have taken up Arms in Defence of our Liberty, our Property, our Wives and our Children," he wrote, going on to announce the arrival of American generals Schuyler and Benedict Arnold, who came "not to plunder, but to protect you." Unfortunately, the Canadians did not choose to join the fight against England.

After the defeat of the Hessians at Trenton, Lord Charles Cornwallis and his 7,000 troops met a smaller American force on January 2, 1777. Cornwallis delayed his approach, however, and Washington led his men around the main British force, attacking its rear guard in Princeton, New Jersey, before slipping away. It was one of Washington's bold, surprising maneuvers, a badly needed victory during the winter of 1777. This painting (below) by John Trumbull depicts a calm Washington in the midst of the battle.

VICTORY AND INDEPENDENCE

In 1777, Washington decided to fight to save Philadelphia, which was being threatened by the British. Sending 3,000 of his troops to Major General Horatio Gates in New York, Washington confronted the British at Brandywine and Germantown, Pennsylvania, only to be beaten. Thanks to the reinforcements sent him by Washington, however, Gates won a great victory at Saratoga, New York, on October 17.

Saratoga was a major turning point. It brought France into the war on the American side. Soon, the French government sent troops, weapons, and money to help the American cause. Despite the good news from Saratoga, Washington and the army spent a rough winter at Valley Forge, Pennsylvania, where the troops struggled to stay alive. Washington fell ill, but Martha nursed him back to health.

In June 1778, the British left Philadelphia and concentrated their troops in New York. Chasing the army, the Americans defeated the British at Monmouth, New Jersey. After Monmouth, the fighting shifted to the Southern colonies. In 1781, British general Charles Cornwallis blundered. Leading his army to the Virginia coast, Cornwallis took up a defensive position at Yorktown. Seeing an opportunity to trap Cornwallis, Washington secretly moved his troops, now reinforced by the French, to Virginia and attacked. On October 19, 1781, after eleven days of shelling, Cornwallis surrendered.

At Valley Forge, Washington's army lacked sufficient food, clothing, medicine, and shelter. In the snowy scene in this engraving from the nineteenth century (right), Washington is standing with his ragged, shoeless soldiers. The figure on the left is the Baron Friedrich Wilhelm von Steuben (1730–94), a German officer who trained the Americans in the use of bayonets and how to maneuver in ranks.

General Cornwallis surrendered his army on October 19, 1781. Furious at Cornwallis's refusal to attend the surrender ceremony, George Washington, seen on the dark horse at the right in John Trumbull's painting (below), ordered his deputy, General Benjamin Lincoln, to direct the British surrender. Lincoln is shown (center, on horseback) leading the British soldiers to surrender their arms as they are marched between the French army on the left and the Americans on the right.

THE PROBLEMS OF NATIONHOOD

When the British surrendered at York-town, a band played a tune called "The World Turned Upside Down." The song fit the occasion. An upstart colonial army had beaten one of the world's foremost military powers. Without the leadership of George Washington, the outcome might have been very different. As a military leader, Washington was bold at times, cautious at others, but he managed to persist through great difficulties. Washington's concern for his men was always uppermost. He never asked them to bear hardships he was unwilling to share.

After Yorktown, Washington urged Congress to maintain the army's strength during peace negotiations. From 1781 until September 1783, when the Treaty of Paris was signed, few battles were fought: The British slowly began to give up control of the thirteen American colonies.

Longing to return to civilian life, Washington said farewell to his officers at Fraunces Tavern in New York City on December 4, 1783. "With a heart full of love and gratitude," he told them, "I now take leave of you. I most devoutly wish that your later days may be as prosperous and happy as your former ones have been glorious and honorable." Shaking hands, his eyes filled with tears, Washington left New York on December 23 to resign his commission at the Continental Congress meeting in Annapolis. On Christmas Eve, 1783, he rode up the long, winding drive to Mount Vernon, home at last after nine years of war.

When the British finally evacuated New York City on November 25, 1783, two months after the signing of the peace treaty, Washington led his men through the city streets (above). A month later, Washington left New York for Annapolis, the temporary home of the Continental Congress, to resign his commission.

Between Yorktown in 1781 and the end of the war in September 1783, Washington established his headquarters at Newburgh, New York, on the west bank of the Hudson River about sixty miles from New York City. He lived in the small house shown in this Currier & Ives lithograph (right).

THE CONSTITUTIONAL CONVENTION

In his retirement, Washington toured the lands to the west and was disturbed to find that frontier settlers felt little connection to the original thirteen states. He began to fear that the newly independent nation might come apart. Under the Articles of Confederation, which governed the nation, individual states regulated their own trade, coined their own currency, and negotiated independently with foreign nations. The national government had very little authority. A 1786 meeting at Annapolis, Maryland, failed to solve the problems facing the new nation. Another convention—known as the Constitutional Convention—was called for May 1787 in Philadelphia.

At first, Washington was reluctant to become involved, but in late 1786, news of the riots of Shays's Rebellion in Massachusetts upset him. "We are fast verging to anarchy and confusion," he wrote to James Madison. Soon afterward he was chosen as a Virginia delegate to the convention.

As the most famous and respected delegate, Washington was selected to be president of the convention. After five days of debates, the delegates voted to discard the weak Articles of Confederation and to draw up a new constitution establishing a stronger national government. In the weeks that followed, Washington quietly expressed his support for "an indissoluble Union of the States under One Federal Head."

While the Constitutional Convention was meeting in Philadelphia in 1787, Charles Willson Peale painted a portrait of Washington (above) as commander in chief of the army and as president of the convention, which was then engraved and made into this seal. Peale painted a series of portraits and full-length studies of Washington at Valley Forge and in later years.

This cartoon (below) by Amos Doolittle portrays the disorder the upcoming Constitutional Convention caused in Connecticut. Titled "The Looking Glass for 1787," it shows the state as a cart stuck in a muddy ditch, being pulled in opposite directions by the Federalists on the left who say, "Comply with Congress," and the anti-Federalists on the right, who shout, "Tax luxury," and "the People are oprest." The cartoon shows other figures making obscene gestures, to illustrate the discord between citizens on the eve of the ratification of the Constitution.

ELECTION AND INAUGURATION

As the debates in Philadelphia continued during the summer of 1787, there was little doubt that Washington was the man to lead the new federal government. On September 17, the new constitution was unanimously approved by the delegates. Ratification (approval) by nine states was necessary for the document to become law, and in June 1788, with New Hampshire's ratification, the Constitution of the United States was adopted.

The popular vote for president took place from November 1788 until January 1789. On February 4, 1789, the Electoral College voted unanimously to elect George Washington as the first president and, as vice president, John Adams. On April 30, on the steps of Federal Hall in New York City, Washington was sworn in before cheering crowds.

Every decision the new president made would establish a precedent for succeeding chief executives. Aware of this, Washington proceeded slowly, using executive power cautiously at first. The heads of government departments originally reported to Congress, but gradually came under the president's authority. Washington was prepared to consult with Congress, but decided the president should not attend congressional debates. Washington also made sure the public saw the presidency as an office of dignity, even accepting the title "His Highness, the President."

Washington agreed to stay in office for a second term. On December 2, 1792, Washington was reelected president, again unanimously.

In this early twentieth-century painting (above) by John Ward Dunsmore, Washington receives the news of his election to the presidency at Mount Vernon with Martha sitting on the right. Washington's feelings, he said, were "not unlike those of a culprit who is going to the place of his execution."

For Washington's first presidential cabinet, he chose Thomas Jefferson (1743–1826) to be secretary of state and Edmund Randolph (1753–1813) to be attorney general. Both men believed in a limited central government. Alexander Hamilton (1755–1804) became secretary of the treasury and Henry Knox (1750–1806) secretary of war. They supported a strong federal government. In this engraving (right), from left to right, are Knox, Jefferson, Randolph, and Hamilton.

WASHINGTON'S SECOND TERM

Washington's second inauguration, on March 3, 1793, was held in Philadelphia, which had become the capital in 1790 and remained so until a new "federal city" was built on land given up by Maryland and Virginia. The permanent capital was named after Washington, who laid the cornerstone of the Capitol building in September 1793.

The most important event of Washington's second term occurred abroad. In 1789, the French Revolution had begun. Two weeks after Washington's second inauguration, French king Louis XVI was beheaded. Soon after, Britain went to war against revolutionary France. Many Americans, including Secretary of State Thomas Jefferson, supported France. Others, like Treasury Secretary Alexander Hamilton, were sympathetic to Britain.

Hoping to stay out of the fight, Washington issued a Proclamation of Neutrality in April 1793. But the British ignored America's neutrality and began seizing American ships and sailors. Washington appointed John Jay to negotiate a treaty to settle the dispute with Britain. When the terms were announced, it seemed that Jay had given in to the British on many points. With misgivings, the president signed the treaty, only to be attacked by the many Americans who sided with France.

Many people urged Washington to remain for a third term as the election of 1796 approached. He refused, however, setting a precedent that lasted until President Franklin Roosevelt's administration in the 1940s.

In addition to negotiating with the British, John Jay (1745–1829; above) held many important public positions, including presidency of the Continental Congress in 1778 and secretary of foreign affairs after the Revolutionary War. Jay declined the post of secretary of state, preferring the job of chief justice of the Supreme Court.

Martha's children and grandchildren spent much of their time at Mount Vernon. Two grandchildren, Eleanor (Nelly) Custis and George Washington Parke Custis, stand near Washington in this Currier & Ives print (right), based on a painting by Edward Savage, 1796. Washington's left hand lies on a map of the North America, while his grandson points to America on the globe in the lower right corner.

The Whiskey Rebellion of 1794 was a protest by poor backwoods farmers against the taxes levied on the whiskey they distilled from their corn. Their anger led them to assault a few federal tax collectors in Pennsylvania and Kentucky. Some of these "Whiskey Boys" were captured, made to sign this oath (right), and then released.

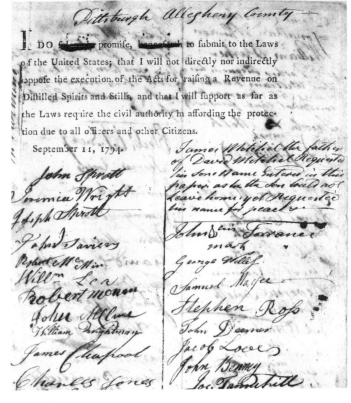

WASHINGTON'S LAST YEARS

Domestic as well as foreign disputes marked the last years of Washington's presidency. Although Washington was opposed to the formation of political parties, his administration split into two groups. The first, the Federalists, were led by Alexander Hamilton. They favored a strong central government that would help the young nation's industries. Others, called the Democratic-Republicans, or Republicans, supported Thomas Jefferson. The Republicans believed that the states, not the federal government, should have more power. Eventually, the conflict grew so bitter that Jefferson resigned his cabinet post.

Returning to Mount Vernon in March 1797, Washington was weary in body and spirit, but the last two years of his life nevertheless hummed with activity. He spent his days writing letters, receiving visitors, and supervising the plantation. On a December day in 1799, Washington rode around Mount Vernon in spite of a cold, sleety rain. He went to bed complaining of a sore throat. His condition worsened, and on December 14, 1799, Washington, the nation's first president and one of its greatest leaders in both war and peace, died at the age of sixty-seven.

Congress requested that Washington's body be brought to the city of Washington, D.C., for burial. Reluctantly, Martha agreed. In fact, Congress never got around to arranging the removal, so the tomb remains at Mount Vernon. This print (above) shows the figure of Lafayette visiting the grave of his former friend and comrade-in-arms.

As his condition worsened and death grew near, Washington asked Martha to find his will. He commented to his doctor, "I die hard, but I am not afraid to go. My breath cannot last long." Martha, seen holding his hand in this Currier & Ives engraving (below), bore his death stoically and said, "I shall soon follow him."

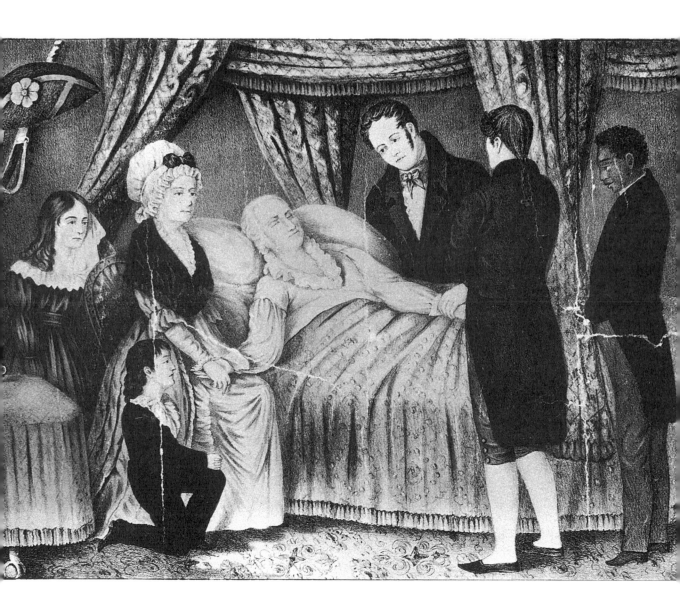

JOHN ADAMS

John Adams was born in 1735 in Braintree, Massachusetts, a farming village just south of Boston. His father was a farmer, a leather craftsman, town selectman, deacon of the church, and a member of the militia. John learned to read by age six. The oldest of three sons, he attended Harvard College to become a Congregational minister. There, he studied logic, philosophy, rhetoric, geography, geometry, and physics. When he graduated in 1755, religion no longer interested him, and he briefly worked as a teacher at a small schoolhouse in Worcester. At this time, he became drawn toward politics and government, and began studying with a local lawyer. Adams's indecision about his profession made him anxious, and he wrote furiously about his self-doubts, fears, and ambitions in his diary. In 1758, he was admitted to the Massachusetts bar, age twenty-three and penniless, but determined to do well.

Adams married Abigail Smith, daughter of Reverend William Smith of Weymouth, Massachusetts, in 1764. He had first met this lively, intelligent woman when he was twenty-three and she was fifteen.

John Adams (1735–1826; above) was America's first vice president and second president. A brilliant political philosopher but often quarrelsome, Adams became known as the workhorse of the American Revolution. He did not always think highly of his colleagues. Of the Continental Congress he once complained, "These great Witts, these subtle Criticks, these refined Geniuses, these learned Lawyers, these wise Statesmen, are so fond of showing their Parts and Powers, as to make their Consultations very tedious." Still, Adams was a firm believer in freedom and representative government.

Harvard College, one of the oldest colleges in America, was organized by the Puritan leaders of the Massachusetts Bay Colony in 1636, who wanted to supply educated ministers for the colony's churches. Harvard was already an impressive collection of buildings, as shown in this engraving (right), by the time the young John Adams arrived in 1751.

John Adams was born on October 30, 1735, at 133 Franklin Street in Braintree, Massachusetts. This photograph (right) shows the room where he was born. Adams described his father, a farmer of modest means, as "the honestest man I ever knew." His mother was a member of a prominent Boston family.

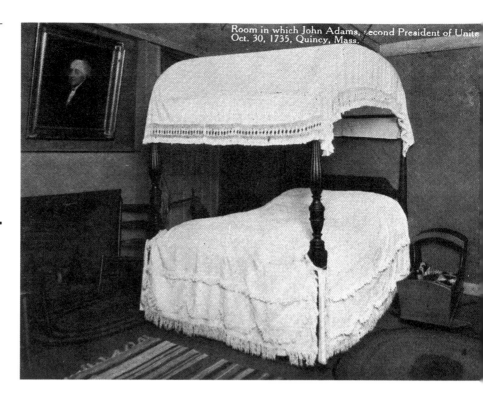

Room in which John Adams, second President of Unite Oct. 30, 1735, Quincy, Mass.

ABIGAIL ADAMS

Abigail Adams is the only woman who was both a wife (John Adams—the second president) and a mother (John Quincy Adams—the sixth president) of an American president. She was born Abigail Smith, into a family that had been involved in politics for generations. Her father was a Congregational minister, but her grandfather had been a representative in the Massachusetts colonial government and was later a Supreme Court justice. Abigail did not receive a formal education, although her father taught her economics, mathematics, philosophy, and the classics, and she read extensively in his library. One of her lifetime interests was the education of women.

When the Adamses married in 1764, they settled on a small farm in a part of Braintree, Massachusetts, that later became Quincy. Five children were born: John Quincy, Thomas, Charles, Susanna and Abigail (Nabby). Although much of their married life was spent apart, Abigail was an intellectual companion for her husband, and she gave him encouragement during his periods of self-doubt. He left home to attend the Continental Congresses in 1774 and 1775, and went to Europe for almost ten years of diplomatic service. During the times he was away, Abigail raised the children and managed the house and farm on her own.

As the wife of the second president, Abigail Adams (1744–1818; above) wished to follow in the footsteps of her friend Martha Washington, although she feared she would never be able to hide her strong political opinions as did "Lady Washington." Abigail also doubted she possessed the "patience, prudence and discretion" of Martha. When Abigail was presented to the Court of St. James in London, she was "elegant" but plainly dressed, and she found the affair a huge bore.

John and Abigail exchanged many letters over a period of years. The range of subjects, moods, feelings, opinions, and events contained in their letters are a unique record of the Adams's marriage and the times they lived through. Although most people viewed John Adams as cold and formal, the letters reveal a man passionately devoted to his wife, whom he called "Miss Adorable," "Best Friend," or "Dearest of Friends." Abigail's witty responses also expressed the loneliness and longing she felt for her frequently absent husband. The original letters are at the Massachusetts Historical Society. But this Little, Brown edition (above, right) is in the Rare Book Division of the Library of Congress.

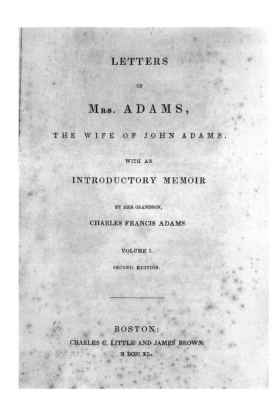

This photograph (above) shows the kitchen in the Adams house in Quincy. Although she was a prominent citizen, Abigail lived modestly and did most of the work of running their house by herself.

Abigail Adams was concerned for the legal rights of women. She admired the English writer Mary Wollstonecraft, who wrote A Vindication of the Rights of Women (far right) in 1792. Abigail would also have agreed with the anonymous female author of this broadside (right) from the eighteenth century, who writes, "[I]f opinion and manners did not forbid us to march to glory by the same paths as the men, we should at least equal and sometimes surpass them in our love for the public good."

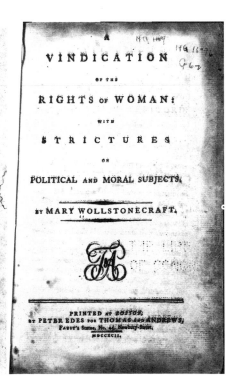

ADAMS AND INDEPENDENCE

John Adams's law practice and family life flourished in the 1760s. In an important case in 1768, Adams defended John Hancock in a smuggling charge. John Hancock was a merchant whose ship was seized by customs agents when they suspected he was defying British trade restrictions by smuggling banned goods into Boston. All charges were eventually dropped. Cases like these drew Adams into protests against British laws and practices.

After the Stamp Act was passed by the British Parliament in 1765, Adams published an essay, "On Canon and Feudal Law," in the Boston *Gazette*, which praised the tradition of English common law because it maintained order and respected the rights of citizens to protest unjust laws. Then, in 1770, Adams defended the British soldiers that were accused of murder in the Boston Massacre.

Adams took a leading role in speaking for the colonists. He was a delegate to both Continental Congresses. He was a key decision maker when the Revolutionary War broke out in 1775, nominating George Washington of Virginia to be commander of the Continental Army. Perhaps his most important accomplishment during this time, however, was addressing Congress on July 1, 1776. Thomas Jefferson reported that when Adams spoke that day, "He came out with a power of thought and expression that moved us from our seats."

The hated Stamp Act of 1765 caused an explosion of anger throughout the thirteen colonies. All newspapers, pamphlets, legal documents, and even playing cards were required to have a royal stamp. John Adams's first act in the struggle against British rule was to draw up a set of resolutions protesting the new law. Forty other Massachusetts towns adopted these "Braintree Instructions." This engraving (above) shows colonists protesting the Stamp Act in the streets.

Adams supported legal protest but he strongly opposed illegal violence, vandalism, or mob rule. When an angry mob of Bostonians began a scuffle with a group of British soldiers on the docks on March 5, 1770, insults and snowballs began to fly. The Americans taunted the British, and as tempers flared, shots were fired, and five Americans were killed. The Boston Massacre is portrayed in this engraving (opposite, top). Adams volunteered to defend the British soldiers in court. He argued so persuasively that they were acquitted of wrongdoing. This action hurt Adams's popularity, and he retired from active political work for two years.

The work of the First Continental Congress was largely directed against the British government's moves to punish rebellious Massachusetts: the closing of Boston Harbor, the appointment of a military governor, the sending of troops, and the closing of the courts. The rest of the colonies knew that what had happened to Massachusetts could happen to them, too. The Congress's first session, shown in this French engraving (right), was held in Carpenter's Hall in Philadelphia on September 5, 1774. It was attended by both John Adams and his more radical cousin, Samuel Adams.

DIPLOMAT AND VICE PRESIDENT

The demands of the Revolution and the new nation frequently kept Adams away from his home and family. He served in Congress from 1776 to 1777 as chairman of the Board of War and Ordnance. He also worked on the Articles of Confederation for the new nation. He yearned to return to Braintree to his family and law practice. In late 1777, after only two months at home, Adams was elected as a commissioner to the court of France. After eighteen months in Paris, Adams returned to Massachusetts where he helped write the Massachusetts Constitution, later used as a model for the nation's Constitution.

Adams returned to France in 1779 to negotiate trade and peace treaties between Britain and the United States. Joined by Benjamin Franklin and John Jay, Adams helped negotiate the Treaty of Paris with Britain, ending the Revolutionary War in 1783. Abigail went to England with him in 1784 when Adams was appointed the first American minister to Great Britain. They returned in 1788. The next eight years were spent in the shadow of President Washington, Adams serving dutifully as the first vice president. Relations between the president and vice president were cordial, but Washington chose not to involve Adams in important questions. Adams viewed the vice presidency as "the most insignificant office that ever the invention of man contrived."

Charles Gravier, the Comte de Vergennes (1717–87; above), was Louis XVI's foreign minister. When the Americans first began the rebellion, Vergennes saw an opportunity to weaken France's chief enemy, Britain. With the approval of the king, he arranged to send arms secretly to the Americans. When Adams arrived in France to seek peace negotiations with the British, Vergennes insisted that Adams's mission be kept secret. Adams suspected, rightly, that Vergennes was not so much interested in helping the Americans win the war as in prolonging it for his own profit.

In the negotiations for the Treaty of Paris, the northeastern boundary between Maine and British Nova Scotia was set at the St. Croix River. Difficulties arose when it was learned that at least two rivers were named "St. Croix." In 1798, when Adams was president, a commission settled the dispute and marked the source of the river with a stone monument, which appears in this engraving (right).

A copy of the last page of the Treaty of Paris with Great Britain, signed September 3, 1783, shows the signatures and seals of the three American commissioners, John Adams, Benjamin Franklin, and John Jay. The terms of the treaty were favorable to the Americans. Britain recognized American independence; specific boundaries were established that extended the country westward to the Mississippi River; and all British troops were evacuated.

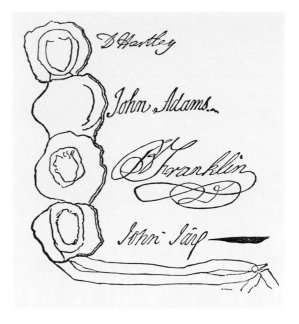

ADAMS AS PRESIDENT

John Adams ran for president in 1796. There were two others in the race: Thomas Pinckney (supported by Alexander Hamilton and the Federalists), and Thomas Jefferson (backed by the Democratic-Republicans). In a very close vote, Adams was elected president by just three votes more than Jefferson, who became vice president. Most of the North voted for Adams, the South for Jefferson.

Adams was a moderate who wanted to balance the interests of both parties. A central issue at this time was the war between Britain and France. Since 1795, both countries had been acting aggressively toward America, seizing hundreds of American ships and sailors. Adams attempted to maintain Washington's policy of neutrality.

In May 1796, Adams sent envoys to France to negotiate for peace, at the same time building up defense forces in America. When it came out that the French foreign minister had attempted to obtain bribes from the American commissioners before agreeing to negotiate, the Federalists began stirring up anti-French feeling. It was called the XYZ Affair. Adams did not declare war, but ordered armed merchant ships to attack French ships. But Adams also continued to seek peace and finally signed a settlement in 1800. He had almost single-handedly avoided war with France, in spite of agitation from the Federalists.

Amos Doolittle's 1799 engraving (right) shows a bust portrait of John Adams as president, surrounded by the coats of arms of sixteen states. The eagle holds an arrow and an olive branch with the motto, "Millions for our Defence Not a Cent for Tribute." This statement refers to the XYZ affair, in which the French tried to extort bribes from the American negotiators in France, and the two countries nearly went to war. Meanwhile, Adams and Congress authorized money to build up the nation's army and navy.

During the last year of Adams's presidency, the national government moved from Philadelphia to the new Federal City on the Potomac River. George Washington had selected the site, and hired French architect Pierre Charles L'Enfant to lay out the city plan, making it the first planned capital city in the world. As this watercolor (below) by William Birch shows, the city of Washington was hardly more than a clearing in the wilderness in its early years. The Adamses got lost on their trip from Baltimore to Washington, wandering for two hours looking for a guide or a path. Not a single room was completely finished in the president's house. Abigail wrote, "We have, indeed, come into a new country."

ADAMS'S LAST YEARS

The 1800 presidential campaign was a bitter one, each party discrediting the other and spreading ugly rumors against both Adams and Jefferson. In the election, Jefferson tied with Aaron Burr, the Federalist candidate. A compromise was reached after thirty-six ballots. After quietly agreeing not to make any radical changes, Jefferson was elected by the House of Representatives, with Aaron Burr as his vice president. It was a bitter loss for Adams, and he refused to attend Jefferson's inaugural, the first held in the new capital of Washington, D.C. In his last act as president, Adams appointed the so-called "midnight judges," all Federalists, of whom John Marshall, as chief justice of the Supreme Court, was the most important.

Abigail and John Adams returned to Quincy, Massachusetts. He spent his retirement years working on his correspondence, rereading the classics, and tending to his personal affairs, enjoying the life of a family man so long denied him. His friendship with Jefferson was rekindled after Abigail wrote secretly to Jefferson on the death of his daughter. The old allies corresponded until the end of their lives. On July 4, 1826, fifty years after the Declaration of Independence, John Adams died, rallying in his last moments to say "Jefferson still lives," not aware that his Revolutionary comrade and political enemy had died earlier that same day.

The third president's election was decided in the House of Representatives after Thomas Jefferson (1743–1826) tied with Aaron Burr (1756–1836). In an all-night session of thirty-six ballots, Jefferson (above) was elected after Alexander Hamilton threw his support to Jefferson as the "lesser evil." Burr became vice president. (In 1804, when the Twelfth Amendment to the Constitution was passed, separate balloting for the president and the vice president was initiated.) Jefferson was the first president to be inaugurated in the city of Washington.

John and Abigail Adams came to live in this salt-box cottage (right) after their marriage in 1764. It is part of the Adams's historical site in Quincy, just a few yards from the very similar cottage where John Adams was born. Adams practiced law here and in 1799 wrote the Massachusetts Constitution in a room that had once been the kitchen.

To many Americans, the deaths of two great men on the anniversary of the signing of the Declaration of Independence seemed to have an almost religious significance. This newspaper, like many others, printed extra editions to mark the passing of Jefferson and Adams.

Metropolitan—EXTRA.

METROPOLITAN OFFICE,
July 12th, 1826.

Scarcely had the mournful intelligence reached us of the death of the sage and venerable father of our Independence, ere a fresh draught is drawn upon our sympathies, for his like venerable compeer JOHN ADAMS. *Jefferson* and *Adams* were twin stars that shone with resplendent glory, during the whole eventful struggle of the revolution. They have descended together to the tomb, and the prayers and blessings of their countrymen follow them. Their services, in conjunction with the happy coincidence of their deaths, have secured them an imperishable niche in the temple of fame. The late anniversary will be hailed as a glorious era in the annals of liberty, and we most sincerely trust will be 'solemnized with pomps, shows, games, 'sports. guns, bells, bon-fires and illuminations,' until the end of time.

It is our greatest gratification to record, that from the moment the melancholy tidings were received, every political feeling was banished; our citizens only remembered that these illustrious men were the promoters of their country's independence, and had hallowed it by their death. Indeed, if the world had asked a sign to prove the *divina origine* of our compact, it would have it in the *miracle* of their simultaneous demise, on the Jubilee of American Freedom.

The very day after our worthy Mayor had called the attention of the Town Councils in his truly feeling and eloquent address upon the death of Jefferson, he had to exercise his solicitude anew upon a like mournful occasion, which he did on Monday last, in the following words.

Mayors Office Georgetown,
10th July 1826.

To the Honorable, the Board of Aldermen and Board of Common Council.

Gentlemen: The Committee appointed by your honorable body, to adopt measures in relation to the death of the venerable *Thomas Jefferson*, met, and were proceeding with the arrangements to comply with your wish, when, this morning, it was announced that his compatriot, the venerable JOHN ADAMS, had also died on the same day. They deemed it respectful and decorous to suspend their proceedings until the Corporation should have an opportunity to express their sentiments in relation to this additional event, so well calculated to excite our feelings.

The character of the illustrious deceased is too well known to you, Gentlemen, and to his country, to render necessary any remarks from me; suffice it, that he was the efficient, energetic, and eloquent compeer of the illustrious *Jefferson*, and, in all that related to invaluable services to our country, his firm and faithful ally.

Very respectfully,
I am, Gentlemen,
Your obt. servt.
JOHN COX, Mayor.

Mr. Addison then introduced a resolution expressive of the high sense which was entertained by the Board of Common Council, and by every American, for the services of these compeers in glory, and a wish, that as in their lives they had been united in the great cause of liberty, so in their deaths the honors due their memory should not be divided. It is needless to add, that it was passed without one dissenting voice.

The Committee to whom was referred the necessary ceremonials, passed the following resolution:

At a meeting of the Committee of Citizens, appointed by the Corporation of Georgetown, for the purpose of adopting measures and making arrangements for paying all suitable respect to the memory of *Thomas Jefferson* and of *John Adams,*

PRESENT

John Cox, Mayor—John Mason—Walter Smith—John Threlkeld—Thomas Corcoran, Sen.—John Laird—William Marbury—Leonard Mackall—Clement Smith—Charles King—James S. Morsell—Charles Worthington and Charles A. Beatty.

Resolved, That a day be set apart (of which due notice will be given) for the observance of such solemn ceremonies, as may evince the deep regret felt for the death, and the high sense entertained of the virtues, the patriotism, and the extraordinary usefulness during the long lives of these highly distinguished men—in which the citizens of the town and of the adjacent country of the district, and the strangers residing in the town and vicinity shall be invited.

That Francis S. Key be requested to deliver an oration on the occasion, at such time and place as shall hereafter be determined on.

That the members of this committee will wear crape on the left arm for thirty days, and that our fellow citizens be, and they are hereby respectfully invited to do the same.

JOHN COX, Mayor,
Chairman.

WALTER SMITH,
Secretary.

Washington sits with his closest advisers, Secretary of State Thomas Jefferson (seated, at left) and Secretary of the Treasury Alexander Hamilton (standing) in this mural in the Capitol building by Constantino Brunidi. The first five presidents worked closely together, frequently serving in each other's cabinets. Jointly they set precedents and made decisions that shaped the office of the presidency.

Thomas Jefferson described the American republic as the "world's best hope." He saw it as a government founded on reason and democratic principles. But the nation was still very young, and its leaders faced many new, unexpected challenges, both at home and abroad

The Constitution was not specific about the office of the presidency, and what exactly a president's powers were. The legislative branch (the Senate and the House of Representatives) was designed as the predominant authority. President Jefferson set a precedent for greater presidential power by authorizing the Louisiana Purchase from France during his administration. This act nearly doubled the size of the country, and opened up the West to exploration and settlement.

When James Madison became president, he inherited a diplomatic challenge presented by warring nations in Europe. These tensions exploded for America in the war of 1812. For the first time, the president was asked to serve as commander in chief of the armed forces. Madison was not very efficient as a military leader, and he received the blame for leading America to war. But the struggle helped reaffirm national pride and identity for the new country.

President James Monroe took this patriotism another step forward and defined America's foreign policy. He and John Quincy Adams drafted the Monroe Doctrine, which made the western hemisphere off-limits to European colonial interests and announced that America would henceforth stay out of all European wars.

THOMAS JEFFERSON: EARLY YEARS

Thomas Jefferson was born on April 13, 1743, in Shadwell, Virginia, where his father farmed tobacco. From his father, Jefferson knew the life of the land-clearing pioneer, but through his mother, a member of the wealthy Randolph family, he also knew the gentlemen farmers of tidewater Virginia. He learned to ride, swim, hunt, and fish at an early age. Reading was another passion.

When Jefferson was fourteen, his father died, leaving him head of the family and manager of his father's plantations. In 1760, Jefferson enrolled at William and Mary College in Williamsburg, Virginia, where he studied languages, science, ethics, religion, politics, mathematics, agriculture, history, and poetry. He wrote, "It is wonderful how much we may do if we are always doing." Young Jefferson also enjoyed plays and horse races, concerts, and dances. He came under the influence of several older men, including Francis Fauquier, Virginia's royal governor, who frequently invited Jefferson to the governor's mansion.

In 1762, Jefferson graduated from college. For the next five years he studied law. After his admission to the bar, Jefferson practiced as a county circuit lawyer. In 1769, he was elected to Virginia's colonial legislature, the House of Burgesses. In the legislature, Jefferson sponsored legislation to prohibit slavery, but it was not accepted.

Martha (Patsy) was Jefferson's oldest daughter and the only child to survive him. When Patsy was eleven, Jefferson laid out a schedule providing for eight hours of study a day: "[F]rom 8. to 10. o'clock, practise [sic] music, from 10. to 1. dance one day and draw another, from 3. to 4., read French . . ." In 1784 he took Patsy to Paris with him, leaving his younger daughter Maria (Polly) in Pennsylvania. Maria joined them eventually. Martha, in this portrait by Thomas Sully (above), was tall and red-haired like her father. She later wrote her memories of Jefferson's loving care of her sick mother during her last illness, and described the paralyzing grief he experienced when she died.

When Jefferson's father, Peter, was named manager of Tuckahoe (below), the estate of his wife's cousin, he moved his family to the plantation, fifteen miles from Shadwell, Virginia, Thomas Jefferson's birthplace. Thomas lived in the elegant house for seven years, taking advantage of a nearby grammar school, the foundation of his formal education. Jefferson's respect for his self-educated father ran deep.

The third president of the United States, shown in this Currier & Ives print (left), was a man of many talents and interests. Jefferson was a musician (he called music "the favorite passion of my soul"), an astronomer, a scientist, a student of languages, an architect, a lawyer, farmer, botanist, philosopher, statesman, geographer, surveyor, and writer. The inscription around the inside of the dome of the Jefferson Monument in Washington, D.C., expresses one of his firmest convictions: "I have sworn upon the altar of God eternal hostility against every form of tyranny over the mind of man."

Martha Wayles Skelton, Jefferson's wife, seen here in silhouette in her only known portrait, was a young widow when Jefferson met her in Williamsburg. Auburn-haired, tall, and slender, she was well educated, a passionate reader, and an accomplished musician. They were married in 1772, and in ten years she had six pregnancies, which took such a toll on her health that she fell ill and died at the age of thirty-two in 1782. Jefferson wrote in his autobiography that when she died he "lost the cherished companion of my life, in whose affections unabated on both sides, I had lived the last ten years in unchequered happiness." He never remarried.

AUTHOR OF INDEPENDENCE

In 1774, Jefferson published an influential pamphlet titled *A Summary View of the Rights of British America.* Jefferson listed the rights granted Englishmen by law and by God and which were being denied the American colonists. He hinted that the colonies might soon break with the crown if their complaints went unanswered.

After fighting broke out in 1775, the split between America and Britain finally occurred. In 1776, Jefferson was elected to the Second Continental Congress in Philadelphia. At thirty-two, he was one of the youngest delegates. Massachusetts delegate John Adams, impressed with Jefferson's writing skill, asked that he draft a formal declaration of independence from Britain. Jefferson responded with the magnificent document that has inspired the world ever since.

After returning to Virginia in September of 1776, Jefferson took the lead in forming the new state's government. Jefferson succeeded in establishing freedom of religion in Virginia's state constitution.

This wood engraving (above) shows Thomas Jefferson's design for the Great Seal of the United States. One side depicts a Biblical scene—the drowning of the Egyptian Pharaoh and his army in pursuit of the Israelites led by Moses. The motto reads "Rebellion to Tyranny is Obedience to God." On the other side, the figures of Liberty on the left and Justice, with sword and scales, on the right, support a coat of arms. The initials of the thirteen colonies encircle the figures.

On July 4th, 1776, the Continental Congress signed the Declaration of Independence and presented it to John Hancock, who presided, as shown in this painting (opposite, top) by John Trumbull. The members of the Declaration Committee are standing in the center. From left to right they are: John Adams, Roger Sherman, Robert R. Livingston, Thomas Jefferson, and Benjamin Franklin.

From June 11 to June 18, 1776, Jefferson worked on his draft for the Declaration of Independence in his room at Jacob Graaf's boardinghouse in Philadelphia. Before submitting it to the convention, he gave copies to the members of the committee, who made very few changes. Next, the delegates read it and discussed it at the convention. Jefferson kept silent during the debate, although he was upset when the delegates agreed to cut out the part of the document that would end slavery. The final, signed version is shown here (right).

GOVERNOR, DIPLOMAT, AND VICE PRESIDENT

In 1779, Jefferson was elected governor of Virginia. In January 1781, the British invaded the state. Jefferson was forced to flee its capital, Richmond, which the British nearly destroyed. Jefferson was blamed for the military disaster, and his conduct in office was investigated by Virginia's legislature. Eventually, the legislature found him innocent of any wrongdoing. Still, the investigation angered Jefferson, and he retired from politics.

Jefferson reentered public service in 1783. A year later, he was elected to Congress, where he drafted a proposal for the government of the new nation's western territories. He also devised a currency system, eventually adopted by Congress.

As minister to France in 1785, Jefferson witnessed the beginning of the French Revolution. Jefferson sympathized with the revolutionaries and helped them form a new government.

In 1789, Jefferson returned home to serve as the United States' first secretary of state. Caught up in a bitter dispute with Secretary of the Treasury Alexander Hamilton over Hamilton's financial policies, Jefferson resigned in 1793. When President Washington refused a third term, John Adams and Jefferson became candidates for the presidency. Adams was elected by three votes, and Jefferson was elected vice president. In 1800, Jefferson again ran for president.

For the most part, Jefferson enjoyed his post as minister to France. He enjoyed the company of John Adams, Benjamin Franklin, and the Marquis de Lafayette, the young French aristocrat who was a close friend and trusted advisor to George Washington. The painting, music, architecture, and sculpture of France thrilled him, as did the fine food and the manners of the people. Jefferson's post also gave him the opportunity to travel throughout Europe. King Louis XVI of France gave him this passport (above).

In 1784, Jefferson, as a delegate to the Continental Congress, wrote his "Report of Government for the Western Territory" which called for the division of the territory in the West. His report led to the Northwest Ordinance of 1787, which set the guidelines by which Western territories were created and later admitted into the Union as states. The territory (right) eventually became Ohio, Michigan, Illinois, Indiana, and Wisconsin.

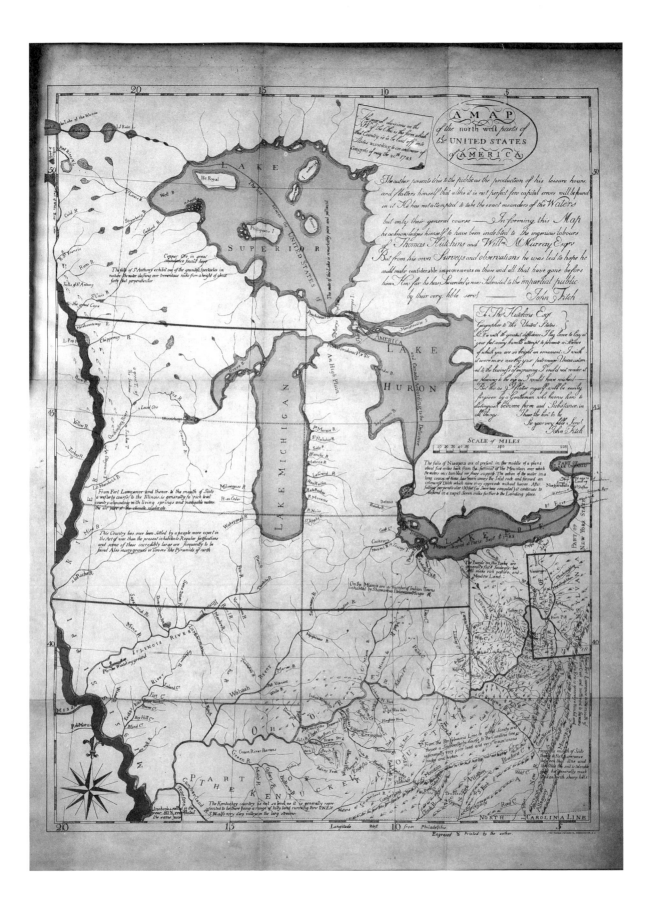

JEFFERSON AS PRESIDENT

The results of the presidential election on December 3, 1800 weren't known until February 17, 1801. A tie between Jefferson and Aaron Burr moved the election to the House of Representatives. After thirty-six ballots, Jefferson was officially elected as the nation's third president. At his inaugural—the first presidential inauguration held in Washington, D.C.—Jefferson stressed the importance of "a wise and frugal government" and "Freedom of Religion, Freedom of the Press, and Freedom of Person."

Jefferson's most important achievement as president was the purchase of the vast Louisiana Territory, which stretched from the Mississippi River to the Rocky Mountains. Spain had secretly transferred the territory to French emperor Napoleon Bonaparte. When Napoleon declared war against Britain, he decided to sell the entire Louisiana Territory to the United States for $15 million (about $2 an acre). The size of the United States doubled overnight.

Reelected in 1804, Jefferson faced growing conflict with England, France, and Spain. War was raging in Europe, although the United States stayed neutral. To reinforce American neutrality, Jefferson proposed the Embargo Act in 1807. The law, which forbade American ships from trading with foreign nations, caused an economic slump in New England. Jefferson's popularity sank. Not wishing a third term, he supported James Madison as his successor.

In this engraving (above) from an 1800 painting by Rembrandt Peale, Jefferson is presented as statesman, writer of the Declaration of Independence, inventor, and president. Jefferson was determined that "Republican simplicity" would be the rule in his White House. He once received British minister Anthony Merry in slippers and socks. The apparatus to the right is an electrostatic machine which he bought in Europe in 1786.

This engraving (opposite, top) shows Jefferson preparing to ride his own horse alone to his inauguration. In fact, Jefferson went to the ceremony in a carriage, but it became his habit, as president, to go for long solitary rides around the outskirts of Washing-ton every day from noon until 3:00 p.m.

In 1803, Jefferson appointed his private secretary, army officer Meriwether Lewis, to the head the exploration party of the newly purchased Louisiana Territory. Lewis chose frontier soldier William Clark to help him lead the expedition of about forty-eight explorers. This 1906 drawing (right) by Frederic Remington captures a moment of rest for the expedition party, which mapped the Missouri River, crossed the Continental Divide in the Rockies, and descended the Columbia River to the Pacific Ocean.

Aaron Burr (1756–1836; left) was a man of many talents. A charming and brilliant politician, he also served with distinction in the Revolutionary War. Jefferson distrusted Burr, however, who served as vice president during his first term. Former Secretary of the Treasury Alexander Hamilton despised Burr. He mounted a successful campaign to keep him from becoming governor of New York. In response, Burr challenged Hamilton to a duel and killed him in 1804.

In 1804, Jefferson negotiated with Spain to purchase West Florida (now Alabama and Mississippi) for $2 million. He wanted to keep the deal secret from the French. These negotiations didn't stay secret for long, as this cartoon (below) by James Akin shows. It depicts Jefferson as a "prairie dog" stung by a Napoleonic hornet, coughing up $2 million in gold coins. A dancing French diplomat waves maps of Florida, saying "A gull for the People." Ultimately, Jefferson failed to reach an agreement with Spain.

Jefferson developed many plans for improving the appearance of the nation's capital. One plan involved planting fast-growing Lombardy poplars on Pennsylvania Avenue up to Capitol Hill. Nicholas King, a surveyor, drew these plans (right) for the trees. Jefferson believed that "The unnecessary felling of a tree [is] a crime little short of murder."

In the competition held for the design of the Capitol building, a mysterious "Mr. A. Z." entered a plan. The anonymous draftsman was actually Thomas Jefferson, who submitted this design (below) for a graceful domed structure. The model for this classical design was the Villa Rotunda near Vicenza, Italy, designed by the Renaissance architect Andrea Palladio.

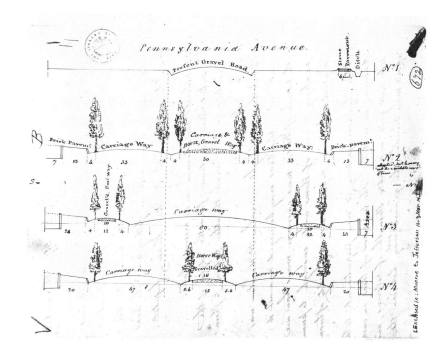

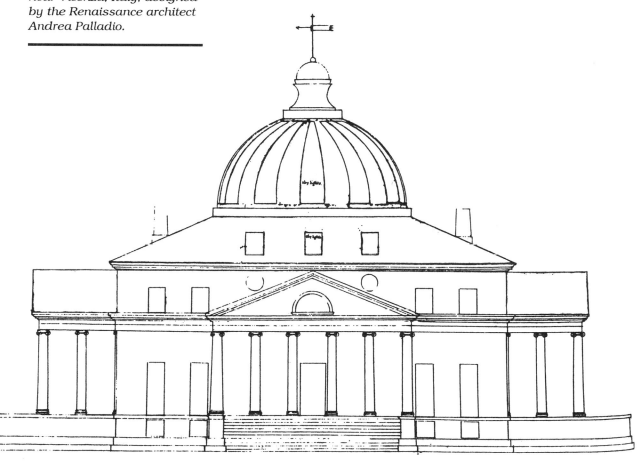

JEFFERSON'S LAST YEARS

After leaving office in 1809, Jefferson returned to the house he had built in Virginia, called Monticello ("little mountain" in Italian), where his many interests kept him busy. His farms, his beloved gardens, frequent guests, and young people to counsel and advise in their studies—all these things filled his days. Most of all, he enjoyed the company of his eleven grandchildren, who lived at Monticello.

A project close to his heart for years had been to find a way to provide public education for all. As a founding member of Virginia's colonial government, Jefferson had proposed legislation for free public education, which failed. He wrote "A Bill for Establishing a System of Public Education," and for over a decade he worked to create a university in Charlottesville, Virginia. Jefferson himself surveyed the land and drafted plans for handsome brick buildings with pavilions, domes, and white columns.

In 1821, at the age of seventy-seven, Jefferson began his autobiography. By this time, Jefferson's health was starting to fail, and he wrote about old age to John Adams: "When all our faculties have left, or are leaving us, one by one, sight, hearing, memory, every avenue of pleasing sensation is closed." On July 4, 1826, Thomas Jefferson died at Monticello. In his will, Jefferson composed the words he wanted on his tombstone: "Here was buried Thomas Jefferson, Author of the Declaration of American Independence, of the Statute of Virginia for religious freedom and Father of the University of Virginia."

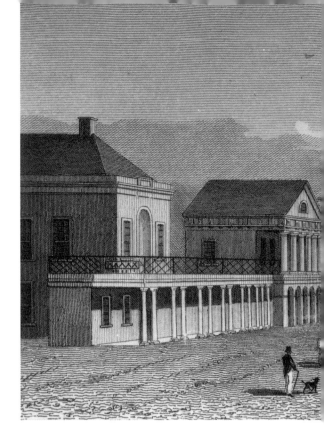

When Jefferson was freed of the "splendid misery" of the presidency, his next project was founding what he called "an academical village"—the University of Virginia. He worked on it for four decades, choosing the site and drawing plans for the buildings, and also organizing a library and recruiting professors. One of the most beautiful of the buildings is the Rotunda, where the library is placed. This engraving (above) from the early 1800s shows the central lawn with the Rotunda in the distance.

As an inventor, Jefferson was both imaginative and practical. Among the many gadgets he designed were a dumbwaiter to bring dishes up to the dining room, a corn sheller, a nail cutter, an apple mill, and a seven-day clock that not only told the time of day but also the day of the week. One of his most ingenious inventions was the "polygraph," which allowed him to make a copy of a letter while he was writing the original. This sketch (right) shows a "spinning jinny," an implement used for spinning thread.

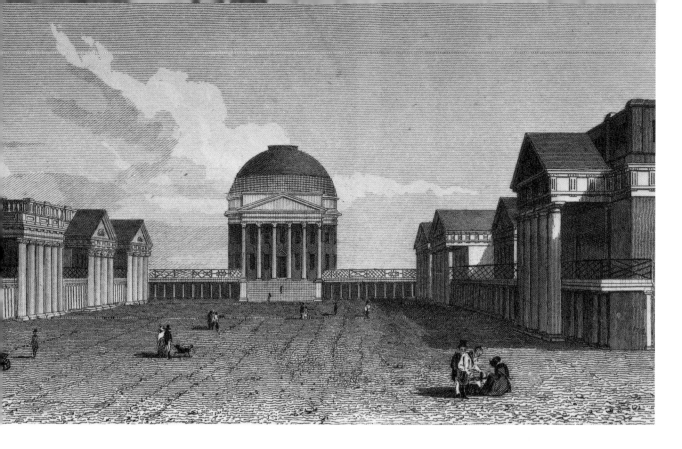

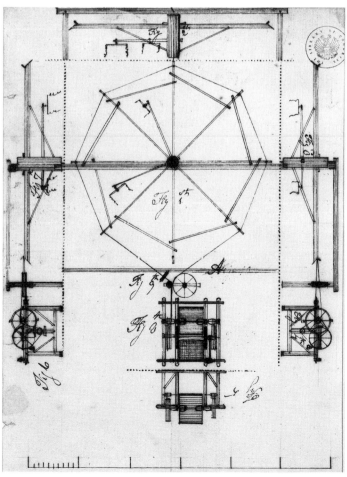

69

Jefferson boasted that he had the best library in America, containing thousands of books on philosophy, literature, architecture, gardening, and science, many of them printed in the several foreign languages he could read fluently. "I cannot live without books," he once said. When the Library of Congress was destroyed by the British in 1814, Jefferson offered his library to replace the volumes. Then he quickly filled up his shelves once again with books like these, bound for him in Virginia.

An engraving from Century magazine (below) shows one of Jefferson's inventions for comfort while reading or writing: the swivel chair (called his "whirligig chair" by his enemies). He also devised a portable writing box, which he used to draft the Declaration of Independence, and a desk that could prop up books for reading.

The house Jefferson began dreaming of in 1768 was his beloved Monticello, a domed mansion built on a hilltop a mile from Charlottesville, Virginia. The interior of the house featured unusually high eighteen-foot ceilings. Outside, Jefferson preserved the magnificent views of the surrounding countryside by placing the outbuildings—kitchen, laundry, storerooms, and servants' rooms—underground, connected by walkways.

JAMES MADISON: EARLY YEARS

The first of twelve children, James Madison, Jr., was born March 16, 1751, at Port Conway, Virginia. James Sr. was a prosperous tobacco farmer, largely uneducated, who was an active citizen in Orange County, where the family moved when James Jr. was a child. Young Madison was a frail boy whose health would never be robust. At eleven, he went away to school and was an excellent student. Unlike most sons of Southern planters, Madison decided to go to college in the North—to the College of New Jersey (now Princeton). Madison studied hard in college, working hours into the night, yet rose every morning at 5:00 a.m.

Although these were years of conflict between Britain and the American colonies, Madison remained aloof from politics until 1774, when he was elected to the Orange County Committee on Public Safety. He also served as a delegate to the Virginia Assembly. Serving on the Committee on Religion, he met Thomas Jefferson, who became his mentor, inspiration, and friend. Together with Jefferson, Madison played a crucial role in the drafting of the Resolution on Religious Freedom, the Declaration of Rights, and the Virginia state constitution.

Elected to the Constitutional Convention in 1780, Madison was the youngest delegate at age twenty-nine. He attended every meeting, quickly realizing that the Articles of Confederation were seriously flawed.

James Madison, Jr., was born in 1751 in Virginia, at his grandmother's home on the Rappahannock River. His mother is shown in this portrait (above) by Charles Peale Polk. Of his mother's twelve children, eight reached maturity, but Nelly Conway Madison's health was weakened by the constant childbearing, and she was often sick. Nevertheless, she lived to be ninety-seven. Nelly loved to read. She taught James Jr. to read and write when he was very young.

Like his mother, James Madison (opposite, top) suffered from poor health, yet lived into old age—in his case, eighty-five. He seems to have suffered periodically from a form of nervous seizure or epilepsy that first struck him while still a child. This ailment made it impossible for him to serve in the army during the Revolutionary War even though he was a colonel in the Virginia militia.

The Madison family's plantation stretched over 1,000 acres up to the edge of the Appalachian frontier. Young Madison was sometimes awakened in the middle of the night by the sounds of Indian raiding parties coming from the forest nearby. This map (right) shows the counties and roads of the settled portion of Virginia in 1751, the year Madison was born.

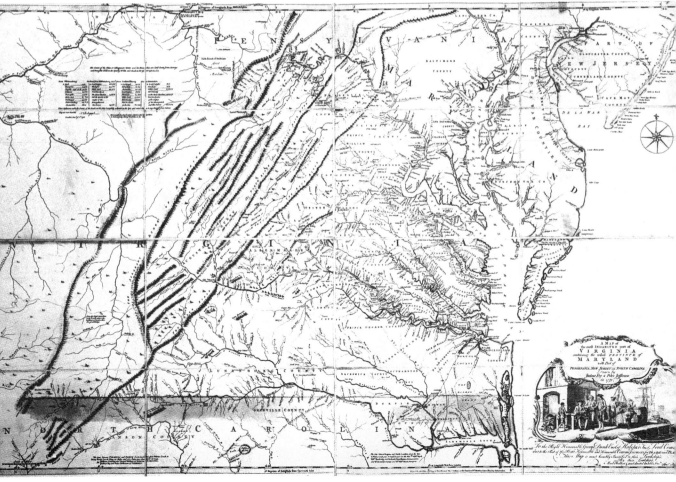

MADISON AND THE CONSTITUTION

Madison's doubts about the effectiveness of the Articles of Confederation grew after the Revolutionary War. Another convention was arranged at Annapolis, Maryland. When only five states sent delegates, Madison, Alexander Hamilton, and other leaders called for a convention of state delegates to reform the Articles.

Madison spent the winter of 1787 studying books on government and preparing an outline for the form he thought the government of the United States should adopt. At the Constitutional Convention in Philadelphia that summer, Madison took part in nearly all the debates. The Constitution was accepted on September 17, 1787. Many of Madison's proposals became part of the document.

Now Madison launched himself into the ratification battle. With Hamilton and John Jay, he published a series of eighty-five essays (twenty-nine of them written by Madison alone), entitled *The Federalist Papers*. The essays explained the principles of the Constitution and argued for its ratification.

Originally, Madison did not think a separate section protecting the individual rights of the people was necessary. Running for election to the new House of Representatives in 1789, however, he changed his mind. Madison took the suggestions of five states and fashioned them into twelve amendments to the Constitution, ten of which became law as the Bill of Rights.

This engraving (right) by John Vallace, based on a painting by Charles Willson Peale, shows the Maryland State House, where the Annapolis Convention took place in 1786. It was held to discuss ways of giving Congress the power to raise money. Madison realized that the selfish interests of each state would "involve this rising empire in wretchedness and contempt."

Before George Washington's inauguration in April 1789, James Madison wrote him this letter (below). It concerns the "Spanish Project," a scheme of the Spanish to bribe settlers to move from American territory into Spanish-controlled lands west of the Mississippi River. Washington, both before and after his election, valued Madison's clear, logical mind and useful advice.

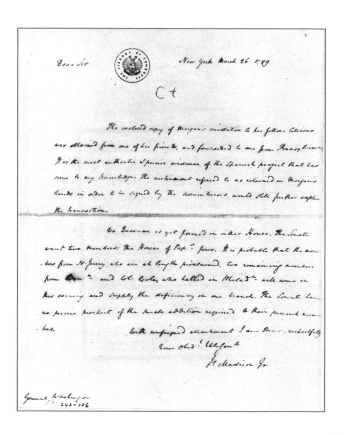

The Pennsylvania Packet *published the text of the Constitution after its adoption in September 1787. The ideas behind the document were largely those of Madison, although the actual writing was done by Gouverneur Morris (1752–1816), a delegate from New York. Along with Thomas Jefferson, John Adams, and George Washington, Madison believed that the true test of representative government was whether or not it "cultivated talent and virtue" among the people. Madison spoke 161 times during the debates at the Constitutional Convention, and came to be known as the "Father of the Constitution."*

CONGRESSMAN AND SECRETARY OF STATE

Secretary of the Treasury Alexander Hamilton's Federalist policies granted great power to the federal government. Madison worried that a too powerful government might destroy the freedoms won in the Revolutionary War and secured by the Constitution.

In 1791, Madison and Thomas Jefferson formed a new party, named the Democratic-Republican Party, in opposition to the Federalists (Hamilton's party). The Federalist-Republican dispute extended to foreign policy. Jefferson and Madison sympathized with the French Revolution and wanted America to support France in its war against Britain. Madison could not accept Washington and Hamilton's support of Great Britain against France. When Jay's Treaty, favorable to England, was made public, Madison left Congress.

In 1798, Congress passed the Alien and Sedition Acts. These laws restricted immigration and freedom of speech, supposedly to maintain American neutrality. Madison responded with the Virginia Resolution, an attack on the acts declaring his belief that states had the right to nullify (declare unconstitutional) federal laws.

Anger at the Federalists' policies spread, and in 1800 Jefferson was elected president. His choice for secretary of state was his closest political ally, James Madison. For the next eight years, Madison advised the president on nearly all matters.

Alexander Hamilton, shown in this painting (above) by John Trumbull, served on Washington's staff during the Revolutionary War, proving himself a capable military leader. After Yorktown, he married the daughter of the wealthy and influential Philip Schuyler, establishing himself in New York society. His political career advanced rapidly, from congressman in the Continental Congress to delegate at the Constitutional Convention, and then to secretary of the treasury in Washington's administration. Hamilton and Madison worked on an economic plan in 1783, but the two men parted ways during Washington's presidency, disagreeing on many political questions.

Patrick Henry persuaded James Monroe (1758–1831) to run against Madison, Monroe's friend and fellow Virginian, for the new Congress in 1788. Neither man campaigned actively. Madison won easily, and Monroe and Madison's friendship continued. As leader of the House, Madison was in an important position. President Washington looked to him constantly for advice. On constitutional questions, Madison's was the first opinion the new president sought during his early years in office. As a Southerner, Madison also mediated between the conflicting interests of North and South. The House chamber where Madison sat, shown in this engraving (right), was in Federal Hall in New York City.

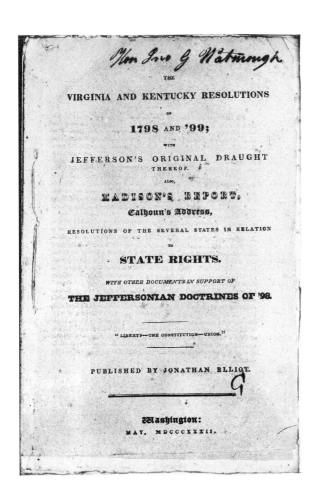

The
VIRGINIA AND KENTUCKY RESOLUTIONS
OF
1798 AND '99;
WITH
JEFFERSON'S ORIGINAL DRAUGHT
THEREOF.
ALSO,
MADISON'S REPORT,
Calhoun's Address,
RESOLUTIONS OF THE SEVERAL STATES IN RELATION
TO
STATE RIGHTS.
WITH OTHER DOCUMENTS IN SUPPORT OF
THE JEFFERSONIAN DOCTRINES OF '98.

"LIBERTY—THE CONSTITUTION—UNION."

PUBLISHED BY JONATHAN ELLIOT.

Washington:
MAY, MDCCCXXXII.

This title page comes from one of the resolutions Jefferson and Madison wrote against the Alien and Sedition Acts. The resolutions argued that individual states could disobey acts of the federal government if they found those acts unconstitutional. The Southern states later used the resolution to defend slavery and to withdraw from the Union.

MADISON AND THE ROAD TO WAR

James Madison was Thomas Jefferson's chosen successor, and in 1808 he was elected president, defeating his rival (Federalist candidate Charles C. Pinckney) by 75 electoral votes.

President Madison inherited a dangerous international situation. France, now led by dictator Napoleon Bonaparte, was still fighting Britain. The British navy continued to seize American ships and sailors. In his inaugural address, Madison criticized both countries, but he hoped trade restrictions would produce a peaceful settlement.

To many Americans, however, it looked as if President Madison was unable or unwilling to fight for the country's rights. When a British ship attacked the American warship *Chesapeake* in 1807, killing or wounding twenty-one Americans, the country seethed with anger. In Congress, a group of young legislators, nicknamed the "War Hawks" and led by Henry Clay (1777–1852) of Kentucky and John Calhoun (1782–1850) of South Carolina, protested Madison's cautious diplomacy.

Feeling he had no choice, Madison reluctantly signed a declaration of war against Britain in June 1812. The first year of the war was disastrous. An American invasion of Canada failed miserably. Detroit was captured by British troops. In spite of the news of American defeats, Madison won a second term in the election of 1812.

When he left Congress in 1797, Madison spent four years at Montpelier with his wife, Dolley. When he returned to public life in 1801 as secretary of state for Jefferson, the capital had been moved to Washington, but the city was still small and lacking in conveniences. This print (below) shows how the Capitol building looked when Madison arrived; the poplars planted by Thomas Jefferson can be seen along Pennsylvania Avenue.

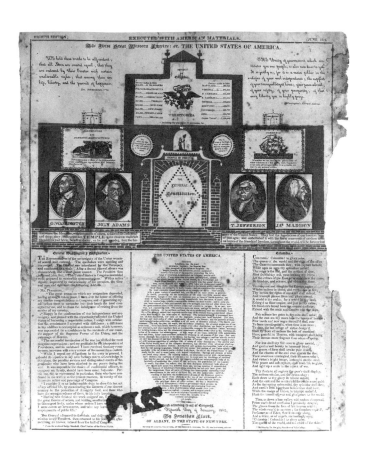

This 1812 broadside (left) portrays various elements of the founding of the American republic. The "Temple of Freedom" is built on the foundation of the federal Constitution. A listing of the seventeen states with their census figures appears on either side of the United States seal. The first four presidents appear in the center. Under their portraits it reads: "[T]he Men who with thousands of others, achieved the Independence of the U. S. They laid the foundations of our freedom broad and deep; they constructed her TEMPLE of the choicest materials of past ages and embellished it with the finest ornaments of modern times."

MR. MADISON'S WAR

The War of 1812, as it came to be known, was called "Mr. Madison's War" by the Federalists and "the Second War for Independence" by the War Hawks in Congress. In mostly Federalist New England, opposition to the war was strong because Britain was the region's chief trading partner.

Although fought over a wide area, the war was small in scale. Land battles along the Canadian border revealed a poorly trained, poorly motivated American army that often retreated under fire. At sea, however, the story was different. Naval battles in the Atlantic and on the Great Lakes included several amazing American victories. Still, the powerful British navy was able to blockade the Atlantic Coast and raid American ports.

The most humiliating moment for the United States came when the British attacked Washington in August 1814. British forces burned the Capitol building and the White House in revenge for the American burning of York (now Toronto) in Canada. In the midst of a headlong retreat by the troops guarding Washington, President Madison himself appeared and tried unsuccessfully to rally the soldiers. Madison returned to the capital to resume his work two days later, never once considering surrender.

A month after the burning of Washington, the British besieged Baltimore but were driven off by stiff American resistance. Suddenly, the nation's military fortunes took a turn for the better.

This political cartoon (right) from about 1813 mocks King George III, who is shown getting a bloody nose by a combative Madison. The United States won several naval victories over the British fleet early in the War of 1812, particularly that of the U.S. frigate Enterprise over the British warship Boxer in September 1813. George III begs, "Mercy, mercy on me, how does this happen!!!" Madison replies, "Ha Ah Johnny! You thought yourself a Boxer, did you—I'll let you know we are an Enterprizing Nation and ready to meet you with equal force any day."

This 1815 British engraving (below) shows the British attack on the city of Washington. British troops assemble in the foreground, watching as flames engulf the capital. Madison's personal determination and courage during the attack was described by an eyewitness: "It was then that the President, who in the midst of all this disorder, had displayed to stop it a firmness and constancy worthy of a better success."

DOLLEY MADISON

Born in May 1768, Dorothea (Dolley) Payne Todd Madison was the daughter of John and Mary Payne, who were Virginia Quakers. In 1783, John Payne moved the family to Philadelphia, only to fail in business, forcing Mrs. Payne to open a boardinghouse. At the age of twenty-one, Dolley married John Todd, a Quaker lawyer. In 1793, an epidemic of yellow fever took the lives of John and one of their two children. Aaron Burr, then a U.S. senator, often stayed at Mrs. Payne's boardinghouse. Burr introduced the widowed Dolley to Madison, and in September 1794, "Jemmy" Madison and Dolley were married.

When Thomas Jefferson, a widower, was elected president in 1800, Dolley Madison became his official hostess. After her husband's election in 1808, she spent eight more years at the White House as "Lady Presidentress." Her lively White House dinners became famous, as did her quick wit and informal manners.

But Dolley shared the hardships of her husband's presidency, too. When British forces attacked Washington in 1814, Dolley was alone in the White House. After repeated warnings, she finally fled. Dolley outlived her husband by thirteen years but remained a well-known and beloved figure in Washington. She died at the age of eighty-one on July 12, 1849.

The first presidential inaugural ball was held in 1809 at Long's Hotel for James and Dolley Madison. At the ball, one guest recalled that Thomas Jefferson's face "beamed with benevolent joy" upon the man (Madison) whom he loved like a son. This portrait (above), painted as a miniature, shows how the future "Presidentress" looked at the age of twenty-six. As First Lady, Dolley held weekly receptions open to the public. One of her innovations, introduced while serving as Jefferson's official hostess, was ice cream. Whatever she chose to serve or wear was instantly copied by the public.

After the burning of Washington, the damage was estimated at more than $1.5 million. Some favored abandoning the city, but others, led by Dolley Madison, lobbied to raise money to rebuild the capital. This engraving (right) shows the gutted White House after the British raid. The troops reportedly ate the food and drank the wine in the White House before lighting the fire, which was put out by a sudden, violent rainstorm. The blackened president's house was repainted to its original white color. From that point on, it was known as the White House.

During the British attack on Washington, D.C., Dolley refused to leave the White House. Finally she was convinced to escape, but not before taking the famous portrait of George Washington by Gilbert Stuart with her, as shown in this engraving (right).

MADISON'S LAST YEARS

In September 1814, an American naval victory on Lake Champlain in New York caused the British to cancel plans for an invasion from Canada. Despite the victory, opposition to the war climaxed in December, when New England Federalists held a convention at Hartford, Connecticut. The Federalists demanded Madison's resignation and even threatened to secede, but he refused to give in.

Since August 1814, American and British diplomats had been meeting in Ghent, Belgium, to negotiate an end to the fighting. Finally, on December 24, 1814, a peace treaty was signed. But one last battle was fought—a brilliant American victory at New Orleans, Louisiana—before news of the settlement reached America.

Madison's term ended with celebrations throughout the country. The war could hardly be called an American victory, but the young nation had preserved its independence and proved its willingness to fight for its rights.

After attending the inauguration of James Monroe in 1817, Dolley and James Madison returned contentedly to their plantation at Montpelier. Madison helped Thomas Jefferson establish the University of Virginia, and then returned to politics in 1829 as a delegate to the convention that rewrote Virginia's state constitution. Madison also worked to end slavery, although he never freed his own slaves.

His health gradually declined and on June 28, 1836, Madison, known as the "Father of the U.S. Constitution," died at the age of eighty-five.

This wood engraving (above) from an 1830 magazine shows Madison's Virginia home, Montpelier. The former president and his wife had no children of their own, but because of his numerous brothers and sisters and Dolley's own two children, Madison's plantation was always filled with young people. Madison also had a large collection of art and sculpture at Montpelier, and he furnished the house with many fine pieces of French furniture.

In 1823, Monroe asked both Jefferson and Madison to comment on a proposed U.S.-British alliance to discourage Spain and France from invading South America. Jefferson now regarded Britain as "the nation which can do us the most harm of any one, or all, on earth; with her on our side we need not fear the whole world." The proposal eventually led to the Monroe Doctrine of December 1823. This letter is from Jefferson to Madison commenting on the proposal in October of that year.

Th.J. to J. Madison.   Oct 1823

I forward you two most important letters sent to me by the President
and add his letter to me by which you will percieve his primâ facie views.
this you will be so good as to return to me, and forward the others to him.
I have recieved Trumbull's print of the Decln of Independance, & turning
to his letter am able to inform you more certainly, than I could by memory
that the print costs 20. D. & the frame & glass 12. D. say 32. D. in all.
to answer your question, Pythagoras has the reputation of having first
taught the true position of the sun in the center of our system & the revo-
-lution of the planets around it. his doctrine, after a long eclipse was
restored by Copernicus, and hence it is called either the Pythagorean or
Copernican system. health and affectionate salutations to mrs Madison
and yourself

Monticello Oct. 24. 23.

JAMES MONROE: EARLY YEARS

James Monroe was the third president from Westmoreland County, Virginia. Son of a farmer and circuit court judge, he was born on April 28, 1758. When James was sixteen his father died, leaving him in the care of a guardian. Monroe's guardian was his uncle, Joseph Jones, a prominent citizen in Fredericksburg, Virginia, and an early supporter of American independence.

Monroe enrolled at William and Mary College in Williamsburg, but when the Revolutionary War began he left to enlist in the Continental Army. He fought in several battles, was wounded at least twice, and in 1776 George Washington personally promoted him to captain for his bravery in the Battle of Trenton.

In 1780 Monroe left active duty to serve as military commissioner for his native Virginia. In Williamsburg, Monroe met Governor Thomas Jefferson, who became a close friend, intellectual mentor, and political colleague. In 1782, Monroe was elected a delegate to the Virginia House of Burgesses and later to the Continental Congress.

When Jefferson went to France in 1784, he gave Monroe a letter of introduction to James Madison. Madison and Monroe soon became friendly. Despite his association with Madison, however, Monroe opposed ratification of the Constitution. He believed it gave too much power to the national government and needed a bill of rights to protect individual liberties.

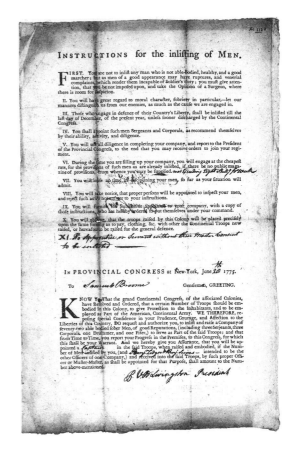

Monroe, who enlisted with the Third Virginia Regiment as a cadet (officer in training) in 1776, was promoted to lieutenant after training at Williamsburg, and distinguished himself in the battles fought at Harlem Heights in New York City, Trenton and Monmouth, New Jersey, and Brandywine, Pennsylvania. He ended his service with the rank of major. This document (above) gives "Instructions for the inlisting of Men" to fight in the Continental Army.

This nineteenth-century engraving (right) shows the disbanding of the Continental Army at New Windsor, New York, in November 1783. Many of the soldiers were angry at the Continental Congress's unwillingness to raise money to pay them for their service. Monroe's departure from the army was a frustrating one. He spent his final years of service as a staff officer, unable to find the field command he desperately wanted.

This lithograph (right) by H. Robinson captures James Monroe's rugged handsomeness. The last of the "Virginia Dynasty" (four of the first five presidents were Virginians) and the last of the Revolutionary War heroes to become president, James Monroe was a solid, effective administrator and a man of impressive honesty and unassuming manner. Jefferson described him as "a man whose soul might be turned wrong side outwards without discovering a blemish to the world."

SENATOR, GOVERNOR, DIPLOMAT

At age twenty-eight, James Monroe married Elizabeth Kortright, the beautiful seventeen-year-old daughter of a retired British colonel and New York merchant. They had two daughters, but their only son died in infancy.

In 1790, Monroe left his law practice for the U.S. Senate. There, Monroe joined the Republicans led by Jefferson and Madison, soon becoming a leader of the party. Four years later, President Washington appointed Monroe U.S. minister to France. Monroe was too openly pro-French, however, and he was recalled in 1796 by an angry Washington. Monroe's strong support for Republican policies won him the governorship of Virginia.

In 1803, President Jefferson sent Monroe back to France as special diplomatic envoy. Learning of Napoleon's offer to sell the Louisiana Territory to the United States, Monroe negotiated a deal. He was overstepping his authority, but he believed—correctly—that Jefferson and Secretary of State James Madison would approve the purchase.

Monroe's diplomatic efforts in Britain and France to secure American rights on the high seas failed, and Jefferson recalled him in 1807. Monroe blamed Madison for his fall from favor, but in 1811, Madison, now president, healed the breach with his friend by naming him secretary of state. Monroe served capably, even taking on the additional job of secretary of war in the last months of the War of 1812.

In this 1875 painting (opposite, top), James Monroe and Robert Livingston (1746–1813) are shown negotiating the Louisiana Purchase with Charles Maurice de Talleyrand Perigord (standing), Napoleon's foreign minister. After dining with Napoleon on May 1, the day before the official purchase was signed, Monroe visited with the Marquis de Lafayette. He presented the French nobleman with the congressional act that granted him a tract of land in the West.

Monroe served two terms as governor of Virginia, the first beginning in 1799, the second in 1811. As governor, Monroe commanded the state militia and was responsible for providing for the state's defense. Until an armory and munitions factory could be completed, the governor had to buy weapons and ammunition from private sources. In this letter (right), Monroe informs the Assembly that a Mr. Lyon Lehman proposes to sell 3,000 rifles to the Commonwealth, but as the governor lacks the authority to "purchase that species of arms" he must make the matter known to the legislature.

The enclosed proposition for the sale of 3000 rifles to the commonwealth was lately received from Mr Lyon Lehman —As the Executive has no power to purchase that species of arms, it did not undertake to deliberate on the propriety of accepting or rejecting the proposal. But as it is connected with a subject now under legislative consideration, and of great importance to the publick, it is thought proper to communicate it to the General Assembly. with great respect and esteem I have the honor to be yr. most obt. servant

Jas Monroe

THE ERA OF
GOOD FEELINGS

In 1816, Monroe won the Republican Party's endorsement for the presidency. The War of 1812 had destroyed the Federalist Party, so Monroe was elected without opposition. Only one electoral vote was cast against him—according to tradition, so that George Washington could keep the honor of being the only unanimously elected president.

With the nation at peace and party conflicts dying down, Monroe entered the White House at a time of national optimism. A Boston newspaper proclaimed the start of an "era of good feelings." Monroe agreed: He believed that the president should be a "Chief Magistrate who ought not to be head of a party, but of the nation itself."

Foreign affairs soon captured the attention of Monroe and John Quincy Adams (1767–1848), his secretary of state and son of the second president. In 1817, Adams negotiated settling the U.S.-Canadian border. In another treaty with Britain the following year, Monroe agreed to joint U.S-British control of the vast Oregon Country in the Pacific Northwest.

To the South, Florida, still ruled by Spain, became a trouble spot. After Seminole Indians attacked Americans in Florida, General Andrew Jackson (1767–1845) invaded the territory. Monroe and his secretary of state opened negotiations with the Spanish, and in 1819 the Adams-Onis Treaty was signed, giving Florida to the United States.

Elizabeth Kortright Monroe (1768–1830; left) is shown in this portrait by Benjamin West. Although Elizabeth's health was never strong, and as First Lady she wasn't able to keep up the demanding social pace set by Dolley Madison, she and James Monroe spent forty-four years of married life together.

In this painting (below) by Clyde Deland, President James Monroe is seen discussing with his advisers the policy later known as the Monroe Doctrine. From left to right, they are Secretary of State John Quincy Adams, Secretary of the Treasury William H. Crawford, Attorney General William Wirt, Monroe (standing), Secretary of War John C. Calhoun, Secretary of the Navy Samuel Southard, and Postmaster General John McLean.

MONROE'S LAST YEARS

Monroe was reelected in 1820, again with only one opposing vote. Before the election, however, the long-suppressed problem of slavery flared up. In 1819, the Missouri Territory, which permitted slavery, applied for statehood. This meant the balance between the slave-holding and free states in Congress would be upset. In 1820, a compromise was reached. Missouri was admitted to the Union, balanced by Maine as a free state, and slavery was forbidden in all territories in the West north of latitude 36'30".

The major foreign policy achievement of Monroe's second term was the Monroe Doctrine. Much of Latin America had won independence from Spain in the early 1800s, but by the 1820s it looked as if Spain or France might try to gain control of the struggling Latin American republics. In an 1823 message to Congress, Monroe proclaimed the doctrine that the American continents were "not to be considered as subjects for future colonization by any European powers."

In 1825, Monroe retired to Oak Hill, his Virginia home. His last years were marred by financial problems and the final illness and death of Elizabeth Monroe in 1830. After moving to New York City, Monroe died on July 4, 1831, aged seventy-three. The country mourned him as "the last of the cocked hats"—the last president who had lived through the military and political struggles of the nation's founding.

During his service abroad, Monroe acquired many pieces of fine French furniture, carpets, tapestries, and decorations. This desk (above) was bought to furnish the United States Legation in Paris. It is now displayed in Monroe's law office in Fredericksburg, Virginia. His inkstand and clock are also on view. In 1906, a collection of letters written by Jefferson, Madison, Lafayette, and John Marshall was found in a secret compartment beneath the first shelf.

Monroe's last months were spent in New York with his daughter, Maria Gouverneur, and her family. He longed to return to Virginia, but his physical weakness prevented any attempt. In April 1831, he wrote the eighty-year-old James Madison, resigning from the Board of Visitors of the University of Virginia. Madison responded with sadness, realizing that he would never see his friend again. Monroe died peacefully on July 4, 1831, and three days later his body was escorted to New York's City Hall, where it lay in state (right).

Before going to France as U.S. minister in 1794, Monroe bought several pieces of land in Albemarle County, Virginia. One was called Ash Lawn, shown here (right), near the homes of his friends—Jefferson's at Monticello and Madison's at Montpelier. Because of his constant attention to public service, Monroe never had time to supervise his properties, and he was, in the end, plagued by debts that grew larger every year. When he left the White House, Monroe sorrowfully sold Ash Lawn.

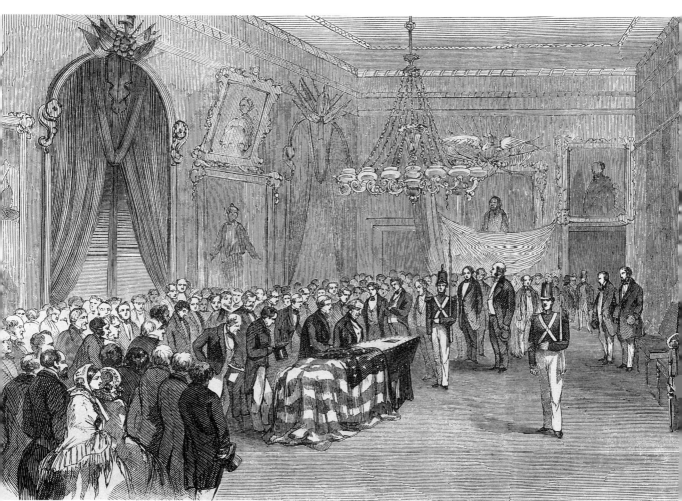

Resource Guide

Key to picture locations within the Library of Congress collections (and where available, photo negative numbers): P - Prints and Photographs Division; R - Rare Book Division; G - General Collections; MSS - Manuscript Division; G&M - Geography Division; HABS - Historical American Buildings Survey
Additional picture sources:
AR - Architect of the Capitol

PICTURES IN THIS VOLUME

2–3 Georgetown, P **4–5** seal, P **6–7** Washington's reception, P **8–9** Map, G

Timeline: **10–11** announcement, P; mill, P **12–13** bank, P; heroes, P; **14–15** Lewis, P; Madison, P, USZ62-36775 **16–17** D.C., P; Andrew Jackson, P

Part I: **18–19** Hall, P **20–21** notes, MSS, LCMSS044-693-130; survey, MSS, LCMSS044-693-85; birthplace, G **22–23** battle, P, USZ62-3913; expenses, MSS **24–25** Patsy Custis, P, USZ61-1498; Martha, P, USZ62-25767; wedding, P, USZC4-630 **26–27** Mt. Vernon, P; farming, P, USZC4-723 **28–29** "le General," P, USZ62-963; commission, MSS, LCMS-44693-71; Cambridge, P, USZ62-23040 **30–31** Naval battle, P; letter, P, USZ62-39590; battle, P, LCD416-698 **32–33** Valley Forge, P, USZ62-57; surrender, P, LCD416-28047 **34–35** Washington, P; headquarters, P **36–37** Washington, P, USZ62-45181; cartoon, P **38–39** election news, P, USZ62-32983; cabinet, P, USZ62-4823 **40–41** J. Jay, P, USZ62-36770; oath, MSS, LC-MSS-95257; family, P **42–43** tomb, P; deathbed, P **44–45** Adams, P, USZ62-45780; birthplace, P; Harvard, P, USZ62-45523 **46–47** Abigail, P, USZ62-3300; memoir, R; kitchen, P, USZ62-55286; Sentiments, MSS; Vindication, P, USZ62-61444 **48–49** Stamp Act, P, USZ62-14365; massacre, P; Congress, P, USZ62-45328 **50–51** Gravier, P, USZ62-45183; signatures, G; monument, G

52–53 Adams, P, USZ62-1798; building, P, USZC4-247 **54–55** Jefferson, P; newspaper, P, USZ62-060776; cottage, P, USZ62-96042

Part II: **56–57** mural, P, **58–59** daughter, P, USZ62-25769; house, HABS; TR, Jefferson, P; wife, P, USZ62-24932 **60–61** seals, P, USZ62-60690; TR, signing, AR; Declaration, MSS **62–63** passport, MSS; map, G&M **64–65** Jefferson, P, USZ62-7583; horse, G; Lewis & Clark, P, USZ62-50631 **66–67** Burr, P, USZ62-24409; cartoon, P, USZ62-28114; Penn Ave, MSS; Capitol, P **68–69** university, P, USZ62-32553; invention, MSS, MS-2774871 **70–71** books, P, USZ62-13902; chair, P, USZ62-38094; room, P, USZ62-24957 **72–73** mother, P, USZ62-33235; Madison, P; map, P **74–75** letter, MSS; State House, P, USZ62-7974; Constitution, P, USZ62-58266 **76–77** Hamilton, P, USZ62-1686; report, R; house, P, USZ62-1686 **78–79** temple, P, USZ62-40915; Capitol, P **80–81** cartoon, P, USZ62-3214; battle, P, USZ62-44919 **82–83** Dolley, P, USZ62-1829; evacuation, G; White House, P **84–85** house, P, USZ62-1829; note, MSS **86–87** instructions, P, USZ62-49633; portrait, P; army, P **88–89** meeting, P; letter, MSS **90–91** wife, P, USZ62-25771; Monroe Doctrine, P, USZ62-10253 **92–93** desk, P, USZ62-11637; house, P, USZ62-32856; funeral, P, USZ62-13819

SUGGESTED READING

BLASSINGAME, WYATT. *The Look-It-Up Book of U.S. Presidents.* New York: Random House, 1984.

DEGREGORIO, W. A. *The Complete Book of U.S. Presidents.* New York: Dembner Books, 1991

MCPHILLIPS, MARTIN. *The Constitutional Convention.* Englewood Cliffs, NJ: Silver Burdett Press, 1985.

SMITH, C. CARTER, ed. *Colonial and Revolutionary America.* New York: Facts on File, Inc., 1990.

SMITH, C. CARTER, ed. *The Revolutionary War.* Brookfield: The Millbrook Press, 1991.

WHITNEY, D. C. *The American Presidents,* 6th ed. New York: Doubleday, 1986.

Index

Page numbers in *italics* indicate illustrations

Adams, Abigail "Nabby" (daughter), 46
Adams, Abigail Smith, 24, 44, *46*, 47, 50, 52, 54
  letters of, 46, *47*
Adams, Charles, 46
Adams, John, 19, 28, 38, *44*, 46, 48-51, *53*, 54, 60, *61*, 62, 75
  birthplace of, *45*
  death of, 54, *55*
  Jefferson and, 68, 60
  as president, 8, 52
Adams, John Quincy, 46, 54, 57, *90-91*
Adams, Samuel, 49
Adams, Susanna, 46
Adams, Thomas, 46
Adams-Onis Treaty, 90
Alabama, 66
Alexandria, Virginia, 20
Alien and Sedition Acts, 76, *77*
Annapolis, Continental Congress, 34, 36, 74, *75*
Arnold, Benedict, 30
Articles of Confederation, 36, 50, 72, 74
Ash Lawn (Monroe home), *93*

Ball, Mary, 21
Baltimore, British attack, 80
battles:
  Brandywine, 32, 86
  Germantown, 32
  Harlem Heights, 86
  Monmouth, 32, 86
  Monongahela River, *22-23*
  New Orleans, 84
  Princeton, 31
  Saratoga, 32
  Trenton, 28, 86
  Yorktown, 32
Bill of Rights, 74
Birch, William, 52
Bonhomme Richard (ship), *30*
Boston Massacre, 48, *49*
Boston Tea Party, 26
Boxer (British warship), 80
Braddock, Edward, 22
"Braintree Instructions," 48
Brunidi, Constantino, *56*
Burr, Aaron, 54, 64, *66*, 82

cabinet, of Washington, 38, *39*
Calhoun, John C., 78, *90-91*
Cambridge, Massachusetts, 28, *29*
Canada, 30, 50, *51*
Capitol building, 40, *67*, *78-79*
  burned by the British, 80
Carpenter's Hall, 49

Chapman, J. G., *21*
Chesapeake (U.S. warship), 78
children, eighteenth century, 20
City Hall, New York, 92, *93*
Clark, William, 8, 64, *65*
Clay, Henry, 78
commander in chief, Washington as, *28, 29*
Congress, Washington and, 38
Constitution, 57, *75*
  Twelfth Amendment, 54
Constitutional Convention, 19, 36, *37*, 38, 76
  Madison and, 72, 74, 75
  Monroe and, 86
Continental Army, 28, 34
  disbanding of, 86, *87*
Continental Congress, 19, 26, 34, *49*, 76
  Adams and, 44, 48
  Jefferson and, 60
Cornwallis, Charles, 31, 32
Crawford, William H., *90-91*
currency system, 62
Currier & Ives prints:
  Declaration Committee, *61*
  Mount Vernon, *27*
  Thomas Jefferson, *59*
  Washington family, *41*
  Washington meeting Lafayette, *33*
  Washington's headquarters, Newburgh, *35*
  Washington's inauguration, *16*
Custis, Daniel Parke, 24
Custis, Eleanor "Nelly", 40, *41*
Custis, George Washington Parke, 40, *41*
Custis, Martha Dandridge, 24, *25*. See also Washington, Martha Custis
Custis, Martha Parke "Patsy", 24

Declaration of Independence, 19, *28*, 60, *61*
Declaration of Rights, 72
Deland, Clyde, *90-91*
Delaware River, Washington's crossing, 28
Democratic-Republican Party, 42, 52, 76, 88
desk owned by Monroe, *92*
Doolittle, Amos, *37*, *53*
Dunsmore, John Ward, *38-39*

eighteenth century, 19, 20
Embargo Act of 1807, 64
Enterprise (ship), 80
"Era of Good Feelings," 90
expense accounts of Washington, 22, *23*

Fauquier, Francis, 58
Federal Hall, New York City, 38, 76, *77*
The Federalist Papers, 74
Federalist Party, 42, 52, 76, 84, 90
Florida, 90
Fort Duquesne, 22
France, 32
  Adams's missions to, 50
  Jefferson as minister to, 62
Franklin, Benjamin, 50, 51, 60, *61*, 62
French and Indian Wars, *22-23*
French furniture, Monroe's, *92*
French Revolution, 40, 62, 76

Gates, Horatio, 32
George III, King, 80, *81*
Gouverneur, Maria, *92*
Graaf, Jacob, 60
Great Britain, *51*
  Adams as minister to, 50
Great Seal, U.S., *60*

Hamilton, Alexander, 38, *39*, 40, 42, 52, 54, *56*, 57, 62, 66, 74, *76*
Hancock, John, 48
Harvard College, 44, *45*
Henry, Patrick, 76
Hessians, 28, 31

Illinois, 62
inaugurations:
  Jefferson, 54, 64
  Madison, 82
  Monroe, 84
  Washington, *6*, 40
Independence Hall, *18*, 19
Indiana, 62
inventions of Jefferson, 68, *69*, *70*

Jackson, Andrew, 90
Jay, John, *40*, 50, 51, 74, 76
Jefferson, Maria "Polly," 58
Jefferson, Martha "Patsy," *58*
Jefferson, Peter, 58
Jefferson, Thomas, 8, 38, *39*, 40, 42, 48, 52, 54, *56*, 57, 58, *59*, 60, *61*, 62, 75, 76, 84
  Burr and, 66
  last years, 54, *55*, 68-71
  Madison, Dolley and, 82
  Madison, James and, 72
  Monroe and, 86, *87*
  as president, *64*, *65*, *66*
  Washington, George and, 20
  Washington, D.C. and, *67*, 78
  wife of, *59*

Jones, John Paul, 30
Jones, Joseph, 86

Kentucky, 8
King, Nicholas, 67
Knox, Henry, 38, *39*
Kortright, Elizabeth, 88, *90*, 91, 92

Lafayette, Marquis de, 32, *33*, 42, 62, 88
Lee, Charles, 28
Lehman, Lyon, 88
Le Mire, Noel, *28*
L'Enfant, Pierre Charles, 52
Lewis, Meriwether, 8, 64, *65*
Library of Jefferson, *70*
Lincoln, Benjamin, 32
Livingston, Robert, 60, *61*, 88, *89*
Louis XVI, French King, 40, 62
Louisiana Purchase, 8, 57, 64,
Mc Lean, John, *90-91*
Madison, Dorothea Payne Todd "Dolley," 78, *82*, *83*
Madison, James, 8, 36, 57, 64, 72, *73*, 75, 76, 82, 84
  Monroe and, 86, 88, 92
  as president, 78, 80, *81*
Madison, James, (father), 72
Madison, Nelly Conway, 72
Maine, 92
maps:
  Northwest Territory, *63*
  United States, 1800, *8-9*
  Virginia, 1751, *73*
Marshall, John, 54
Maryland State House, 74, *75*
Mason, George, 26
Massachusetts, 8
Michigan, 62
"midnight judges," 54
Mississippi (state), 66
Mississippi River, 8
Missouri Territory, 92
Monroe, Elizabeth Kortright, 88, *90*, 91, 92
Monroe, James, 8, 57, 76, 86, *87*, 88, *89*, 92-93
  as president, 90, *91*
Monroe Doctrine, 57, 84, *85*, 91, 92
Monticello (Jefferson home), 68, *71*
Montpelier (Madison home), *84-85*
Morris, Gouverneur, 75
Mount Vernon (Washington home), 20, 26, 27, 42

Napoleon Bonaparte, 64, 78, 88
neutrality policy, 40, 52, 64, 76
Newburgh, Washington's headquarters, 34, *35*
New Jersey, 8

New York City, 28, 34, 38
  Federal Hall, 76, 77
  Monroe's death, 92, *93*
New York State, 8, 32
Northwest Territory, 62, *63*

Oak Hill (Monroe home), 92
Ohio, 62
Oregon Country, 90

Palladio, Andrea, 67
Payne, John and Mary, 82
Peacefield (Adams home), 54, *55*
Peale, Charles Willson, *36*, 75
Peale, Rembrandt, *64*
Pearson, Richard, 30
Philadelphia, 26, 36, 38, 40
  Carpenter's Hall, *49*
  Constitutional Convention, Independence Hall, *18*, 19
Pinckney, Charles C., 78
Pinckney, Thomas, 52
political parties, 42
Polk, Charles Peale, *72*
Pope's Creek, Virginia, *21*
Presidential elections, *38-39*
  1796, 52, 62
  1800, 54, 62, 64
  1808 and *1812*, 78
  1816, 90
  1820, 92
Proclamation of Neutrality, 40

Quincy, Massachusetts, Adams home, *47*, 54, *55*

Randolph, Edmund, 38, *39*
Remington, Frederic, *65*
Republicans. *See* Democratic-Republican Party
Resolution on Religious Freedom, 72
Revolutionary War, 8, 19, 26, 28, *29*, *30*, *31*, *32-33*, 34, 48, 50, 86
Robinson, H., *87*
Roosevelt, Franklin D., 40

Savage, Edward, *41*
Schuyler, Philip, 28, 30
Seminole Indians, 90
Serapis (British warship), *30*
Sherman, Roger, 60, *61*
slavery, 84, 92
Smith, Abigail, 44, 46. *See also* Adams, Abigail Smith
Southard, Samuel, *90-91*
"Spanish Project," 74
Stamp Act, *48*
Stearns, J. B., *25*, *26-27*
Steuben, Baron Friedrich Wilhelm von, *31*
Stuart, Gilbert, *83*
Sully, Thomas, *58*
surveying, 20, *21*

Talleyrand Perigord, Charles Maurice de, 88, *89*
Tennessee, 8
territorial changes, *8-9*
Todd, John, 82
tomb of Washington, *42*
Treaty of Alliance, *28*
Treaty of Paris (1783), 8, 34, 50, *51*
Trumbull, John, *31*, *32-33*, 76
Tuckahoe (Jefferson home), *58*
Twelfth Amendment, 54

United States, map, *8-9*
University of Virginia, *68-69*, 84

Vallace, John, *75*
Valley Forge, *31*, 32
Vergennes, Comte de, *50*
vice presidency, Adams and, 50
Virginia, 62, *73*, 88
  constitution, 60, 72, 84
Virginia Resolution, 76

"War Hawks," 78, 80
War of 1812, 57, 78, *80-81*, 84
  Monroe and, 88
Washington, Augustine, 20, 21
Washington, Augustine, Jr., 20
Washington, D.C., 40, *52-53*, 64, *67*, *78-79*
  burned by the British, *80-81*, 82, *83*
Washington, George, *6*, 19, 20-21, *41*, *56*, 57, 75, 90
  Adams and, 48, 50
  capital city and, 52
  Constitutional Convention and, *36*
  family life, *25*, *26*, *27*
  last years, 42, *43*
  Madison and, 74, 76
  military career, 22, *23*
  Monroe and, 86, 88
  as president, *38-39*, 40
  Revolutionary War and, 28, *29*, *31*, 32, *33*, 34, 35
Washington, Jane, 20
Washington, Lawrence, 20
Washington, Martha Custis, 24, *25*, 26, 32, *39*, 40, *41*, 42, *43*, 46
Washington, Mary Ball, 21
West, Benjamin, *90*
Whiskey Rebellion, *41*
White House, burned by the British, 80, 82, *83*
Wirt, William, *90-91*
Wisconsin, 62
Wollaston, John, *24*
Wollstonecraft, Mary, 47
women's rights, 47

XYZ Affair, 52